CINCINNATI
WINE

···

AN EFFERVESCENT HISTORY

CINCINNATI
WINE

....

AN EFFERVESCENT HISTORY

DANN WOELLERT

AMERICAN PALATE

Published by American Palate
A Division of The History Press
Charleston, SC
www.historypress.com

Front cover images, clockwise: Longworth's Sparkling Catawba. *Public Library of Cincinnati & Hamilton County*; Catawba grapes at Meranda-Nixon vineyards. *Photo by author*; Meier Longworth Commemorative Sparkling Wine. *Photo by author*; Vinoklet vineyard sunset, *Photo by author*.

Back cover images: Catawba putti. *Public Library of Cincinnati & Hamilton County*. Sweet Catawba wine label. *Author's collection*.

First published 2021

Manufactured in the United States

ISBN 9781467148320

Library of Congress Control Number: 2021943430

Notice: The information in this book is true and complete to the best of our knowledge. It is offered without guarantee on the part of the author or The History Press. The author and The History Press disclaim all liability in connection with the use of this book.

To Jenn, my favorite wine connoisseur.

CONTENTS

ACKNOWLEDGEMENTS

I am grateful for the outstanding support of the following history geeks and winos: Paul Ruffing of Green Township Historical Society; Gregory Kissel of the Westwood Historical Society; Mark Schmidt of Monte Cassino Bed and Breakfast; Alan March of the Delhi Historical Society; Jill Beitz of the Cincinnati Historical Society Library; Chris Smith of the Public Library of Cincinnati and Hamilton County; Seth and Maura Meranda of the Meranda-Nixon Winery; Joe Henke of Henke Winery; Kresco Mikulic of Vinoklet Winery; Stephanie Moore of Meier Winery; Mark Ramler, Camp Springs Kentucky historian; Dave Zelman, Riverside historian; Don Perry, Wolfangel descendant; Dustin Heinemann of the Heinemann Winery; Michelle Smith of the Chancery Archives of the Archdiocese of Cincinnati; Jan Flieschmann of the Delaware County Historical Society; Diane Hodges of the George Campbell House—Arts Castle; Jeffrey Burden at Friends of Shockoe Hill Cemetery; Bob Brandstetter; Linda Stevens; George Husmann, expert historian; Katy Holmer, Detuscheim State Historic Site, Hermann, Missouri; Judy Gardner, administrator of St. Stephen Catholic Church; Amy McCoy Glover of Ohio History Connection; Don Heinrich Tolzmann of the German Heritage Museum; Frank Baermann of Weingut Baermann, Merdingen, Germany; Dr. Andrew Feight of Shawnee State University; the Kenton County Library Local History Department, Covington, Kentucky; the Archives of St. Vincent Monastery, Latrobe, Pennsylvania; Missouri State Tourism; Peter Maxson, Flagg descendant; Alice Herfurt, Mullane descendant; Bob Bartlett of the Madeira Historical Society at the Miller House Museum; Richard Tefft of the North East Pennsylvania Historical Society; and the Miami University Rare Archives Library.

INTRODUCTION

The history of Cincinnati wine is a very personal one for me. It's implanted in my DNA. The Catawba grape will forever be synonymous with the odd Cincinnati millionaire Nicholas Longworth. My great-great-great-grandfather John Wiggins Flora sued the Longworth estate in 1894, claiming to be the illegitimate son of Nicholas's daughter, Eliza Longworth Flagg, both of whom by then were no longer living. In the trial, he recounted visiting Longworth at his home as a boy and even getting a tour of one of Longworth's wine cellars. By the time my ancestor was born in 1822, Longworth had already made his millions and had started his hobby of winemaking in the hills of Delhi, on Cincinnati's West Side. Longworth solicited help in the kingdom of Baden-Wuertemburg by placing recruiting ads in newspapers in wine country along the Rhine River, bringing Germanic immigrant tenant labor to work his vineyards and make his wine. Longworth turned a hobby into an industry. He bought the house called Belmont (now the Taft Museum of Art), which became ground zero for Cincinnati winemaking during the Catawba Craze he created from the 1840s to the end of the 1860s.

If John Flora's claims are true, and they've not been disproven, then I am both a descendant of Nicholas Longworth and one of his first Germanic immigrant tenants, Johann Baermann. My great-great-great-great-great-grandfather Johann Baermann left his family's winery in Merdingen, near Freiburg in the Black Forest winemaking region, to come to Cincinnati's West Side to work in Longworth's vineyards. His first farm was in Price Hill, and his son later owned a farm at the end of Palisades Drive in Delhi. The family still runs Weingut Baermann in Merdingen, Germany, to this day. Johann's daughter, my great-great-great-great grandmother Anna Baermann, married an immigrant vineyardist from Baden-Wuertemburg, Joseph Brosey, who made seven hundred gallons of wine in 1860 and two hundred gallons in 1850, in Delhi Township. And like many Cincinnati winemaking families, they intermarried for many generations. Johann Baermann's granddaughter Louise Baermann married prize winemaker Sebastian Rentz's son Sebastian Jr. His other granddaughter, Clara Baermann, married Fred Stetter Jr., the baron of Cincinnati Catholic altar wine.

Like thousands of Cincinnatians, I got my first pair of eyeglasses from Thoma Opticians, owned by the grandson of a Lick Run pioneer winemaker from Baden, Sebastian Thoma. In college, I went to parties at apartments on the former grounds of the Bogen vineyards and at the Williamsburg Apartments in Hartwell. During college, I drank the homemade wine of my engineering classmate Matteo, whose Italian immigrant father made wine in Parma Heights. I made a sparkling mead after college that received an honorable mention at the Miami Valley Homebrew competition. It was no Longworth Golden Anniversary Sparkling Catawba, but it didn't explode in my parents' cellar like Longworth's did—and I didn't need to import French Champagne experts to make it for me. In my twenties, I rented a house on the land that was on the Logan plot of Longworth's Columbia-Tusculum vineyards from Evelyn Wolfengel, a descendant of Gottfried Wolfangel, one of his original immigrant tenants of that vineyard. My favorite morning coffee house, Mad Llama in Madisonville, is on the site of the Cornuelle Ives grape vineyard. Christian Schniecke, Longworth's favorite and most successful vine dresser, is buried two plots over from my paternal great-grandparents at Spring Grove Cemetery.

As a product manager by profession, I'm drawn to the Cincinnati wine story because it's a product development story. Winemaking and grape growing are not for the faint of heart. It took great passion and perseverance to be successful. Success was about choosing the right grape, one that was both sustainable and profitable and that could be made into a good wine. A lot of product research was needed to learn how best to cultivate the native American grapes and make good wines of them. It was about mitigating risk and diversifying your vineyard with a variety of grapes that weathered the seasons differently. And we had one of the best marketing agencies whose coattails could be ridden: Nicholas Longworth, King Catawba.

I want to go back in time and wring Longworth by the neck, leading him through a design of experiments on vineyards and grapes other than the Catawba. I want to have a Scrum meeting with the Cincinnati Horticultural Society, Longworth and his stubborn immigrant growers. I want to start a social media backlash against Thomas Yeatman and his badmouthing of the industry in 1864. I want to do a SurveyMonkey online survey or host an in-person market research session with the Germans who frequented the Over-the-Rhine coffee houses where wines were served. But alas, there is no time machine.

Cincinnati's contribution to viticulture was not the Catawba, but rather the Ives grape, which was cultured here and is still used in U.S. winemaking. Although the Catawba is also used and even still grown within fifty miles of the city, it did not originate here; it was imported from Maryland, and the majority of it is now grown on the Lake Erie Island vineyards. It did become America's first drinkable native wine. But drinkable doesn't translate into award winning or popular. Longworth improved it by making it into a sparkling wine that he promoted voraciously around the world, one that brought Cincinnati the nickname of "Rhineland of America."

Longworth was both a blessing and a curse. He was the biggest grower but surely not the most prolific, nor the first to make sparkling wine. He pumped nearly $500,000 (in mid-nineteenth century dollars) into an industry that gave employment to thousands of immigrants and contributed to Cincinnati's development. He was a curse because he put all his eggs in the Catawba grape basket, badmouthing grapes like the Norton, which would go on to become the backbone of wine industries in Missouri. He is responsible for our wine industry's zenith but also for its eventual demise. He created an industry that was largely dependent on his wine house, and when it was gone, so was the largest market for growers, who didn't have the financial means or social connections to guerrilla market for themselves like Longworth did. Indeed, the demise of our local industry was not because of seasonal rot, the phylloxera or losses of vineyardists during the Civil War—it was because of the closing of the Longworth Wine House.

John Wiggins Flora, who sued the Longworth estate in 1894, claiming to be the illegitimate son of Eliza Longworth Flagg, Nicholas Longworth's daughter. *Courtesy of the author.*

The Catawba could have worked, but it was laborious and time consuming. A grower would have to have great passion for the constant care and maintenance of a Catawba vineyard, forever fighting with the weather. It was a lot easier for growers after the Longworth Wine House closed in 1869 to switch to more consistent and predictable crops like fruit, vegetables and flowers, as most of the growers in Cincinnati did. But if it wasn't for Cincinnati, and our experiments with wine, there would really be no California or American wine industry. Longworth's feud over the Norton grape with George Husmann of Hermann, Missouri, strengthened their knowledge, which Husmann would take with him to California to further propagate their vineyards and grape knowledge. A great torch was passed from Cincinnati.

Most of Cincinnati's published wine history centers on Longworth and the Catawba. But like a good wine, there's a complex and rich history of the other local growers, like the Bogens, the Werks, Yeatman, Buchanan, Thompson, Corneau and many others. There are the untold stories of the hundreds of poor Germanic *vignerons* who came to Cincinnati for a better life. These great stories make up the full-bodied history of Cincinnati wine. Journey with me as I take a knee-deep dive into a hogshead of wine history, crushing some myths and squeezing out the juice of some great Cincinnati grape stories.

NICHOLAS LONGWORTH

THE MAKING OF KING CATAWBA

To begin the story of Cincinnati wine, we need to start with King Catawba, the Western Bacchus, the Father of American Wine: Nicholas Longworth. As far as Cincinnati wine goes, he was the sun around which all winegrowers orbited. Dr. Charles Cist (1792–1868), a historian and German-speaking Russian immigrant to Cincinnati, provided the best contemporary description of Nicholas Longworth:

> *Mr. Longworth is a problem and a riddle; a problem worthy of the study of those who delight in exploring that labyrinth of all that is hidden and mysterious, the human heart, and a riddle to himself and others. He is a wit and humorist of a high order; of keen sagacity and shrewdness in many other respects than in money matters; one who can be exact to a dollar, and liberal, when he chooses, with thousands, of marked peculiarity and tenacity in his own opinions, and yet of abundant tolerance to the opinions, however extravagant, of others—a man of great public spirit, and sound general judgement. All these things rarely accompany the acquisition and the accumulation of riches.*

If not for Nicholas Longworth's Tory ancestry, we would never have known him or ever heard of the Catawba grape. He would have sank into stable colonial life in Newark, New Jersey, as a cobbler, his early apprenticeship, and never left to seek his fortune. Nicholas's father, Thomas Longworth, was regent to King George III of England in Newark. He had been labeled a

Robert Duncanson painted this portrait of his patron Nicholas Longworth in 1858 in front of his gardens and Garden of Eden vineyards, with a Catawba grape cluster cascading off the side table. *Courtesy of the University of Cincinnati Art Collection.*

traitor by the new Americans for his unfortunate profession. By the time of Nicholas's birth in 1784, the family's fortune had been greatly depleted by fines and property confiscations.

As a teenager, then, Nicholas went to Beaufort County, South Carolina, in St. Luke's Parish, to join his two elder brothers, Archibald and Joseph, to find his fortune. Archibald owned a rice plantation with one hundred slaves called Tipperary on the May River Neck, now part of the Palmetto Bluff Game Preserve. Joseph owned Mount Pleasant Plantation, a rice plantation, with seventy-two slaves. Family lore says that Nicholas spent two years clerking at Archibald's plantation store, where he learned to hate the American slave system. He also made a mental note of the farmers he saw growing wild native grapes.

Longworth decided that the West, not the South, was where he'd find his fortune. After a brief return to Newark, he floated down the Ohio to Cincinnati by flatboat. He stayed at the home of Judge Jacob Burnet, a former neighbor of his parents back in Newark who still respected them and their son's right to a better future. Nick learned to practice law, shortly being admitted to the Ohio bar. He accompanied Burnet on up to sixty-mile circuit rides by horseback.

Longworth met a young widow, Susan Howell Conner, at an artists' reception in Cincinnati. Through Susan's help, Longworth erased the stain of Loyalism, "for even a Tory, when in love, may develop into a Republican." He married her in Cincinnati on Christmas Eve 1807. Their children were Mary Longworth Stettinius, Joseph Longworth, Eliza Longworth Flagg and Catherine Longworth Anderson.

Nick became known as the lawyer who would take land for his services, and it was not long before he had accumulated such a vast estate that he was able to give up law in 1818 to devote his entire time to the management of his property and his passionate hobby: horticulture.

The Longworth family lived at a small two-story log house, built during the pioneer period, that they called Rose Cottage, near the corner of Pike and Congress Streets. With pressure from Susan, in 1831 they bought the stately mansion called the Belmont at Pike Street, now the Taft Museum of Art. This would allow them the venue to entertain important guests and house their growing family.

Mrs. Longworth's African American hairdresser, Eliza Potter, provided our most detailed account of the Longworth house and gardens on the eve of their fiftieth wedding anniversary in 1857:

Never again do I expect to witness in this city, or perhaps anywhere, such a scene as I saw that night. There was an immense number assembled;… Tables were set in two large rooms that opened into each other; they were elegantly and beautifully spread, filled with every delicacy, and all kinds of wine.

Then she described the gardens around the house:

You might spend many days in going over this house and the grounds, and always find many things to attract your attention. Although the house is situated in the most fashionable part of the city, the enclosure contains twelve or fifteen acres. You can there find rare flowers and fruits from every clime. While wandering through these grounds one can scarcely believe he is in the heart of a great city. Here are three or four handsome green houses; a large fish pond, with a fountain continually playing in it; a gardeners house; a warren for rabbits; a house for pigeons and one for bees; and if you descend along the graveled walk, lined on each side with wild flowers, you come to a large vineyard of the choicest of grapes.

That vineyard was the local laboratory for native vines and the embryo of the American wine industry. The Sparkling Catawba served that night would become the Golden Anniversary known worldwide.

Longworth and His Wine

The first grape that Longworth cultivated was the Cape or Alexander grape in 1823 in Delhi:

I put a German vine dresser on a hill, on Bold Face Creek, about one mile and a half from the river, and four miles from the city. I planted, in the first instance, the Vevay grape only [known as the Cape variety], *gathered the grapes as soon as ripe, put them on the press as soon as gathered; and from them made a wine of the color of Madeira, and resembling Madeira of the second quality. I added from ten to sixteen ounces of sugar to the gallon of must, and after fermentation, brandy, as is customary with Madeira.*

That first tenant was Johann Paul Amman (1775–1849), an immigrant from Sasbach am Kaiserstuhl on the Rhine River. He and his wife, Rosa, as well as their children—Johann Felix, Johann George, Conrad, Lawrence and Elizabeth—immigrated in 1817 in a treacherous eighty-six-day trek across the Atlantic on the ship *Hope*, during which nearly a quarter of the passengers died. They lived in Philadelphia for several years before trekking on to Cincinnati in 1820. Longworth in 1823 put Amman in the care of a four-acre vineyard on Bold Face Creek in Delhi to grow the Cape grape. He had the bright idea to make a white wine from the Cape, instead of the red wine the Swiss immigrants in Vevay, Indiana, had made. What he got was a white wine similar to the Madeira, a wine that required fortification with sugar and brandy. Longworth didn't see this as a commercial wine and soon gave up the Cape in favor of the Catawba.

Amman continued as a vineyard tenant for a decade, but after his wife's death in 1837, he remarried a woman named Therese, moved and bought a farm in Greenville Township, Darke County, Ohio. He was unlucky there, losing his entire vineyard to rot and pestilence, divorcing his wife and moving back to Cincinnati. He again became a tenant of Longworth's on a small plot next to his original farm in Delhi, where his daughter Elizabeth and her husband, Herman Thesse, were now tenants.

Amman's son Johan Felix (born in 1798) lived on Longworth's Bald Hill vineyards in Columbia-Tusculum at the time of Longworth's death and is buried at Madisonville's Odd Fellows Cemetery along with many East Side growers of the Ives grape.

Longworth fondly remembered Amman in a tribute after his death in 1849: "My oldest vine-dresser, Father Amman, has gone the way of all flesh, and I regret his end. He was a worthy old man." Father Amman was buried at the Delphi Universalist Cemetery, where other Longworth tenant families, such as the Mottiers and Schnieckes, were buried before being moved to Spring Grove Cemetery after the congregation folded in 1872.

Finding the Catawba

After his disappointing results from the Cape, Longworth in 1825 found the Catawba, in the form of cuttings from Major John Adlum of Washington, D.C. Longworth became aware of Adlum due to his book published in 1823, *A Memoir on the Cultivation of the Vine and the Best Mode of Making Wine*, which celebrates native American varieties and urges the planting of vineyards. In a letter to Longworth, Adlum famously said, "In introducing this grape [Catawba] to public notice, I have done my country a greater service than should I have done had I paid the National Debt." The statement is certainly true for Cincinnati. If Adlum hadn't promoted the Catawba, Longworth never would have heard of it or tried growing it and Cincinnati's Catawba Craze never would have happened.

Adlum had found the grape growing in 1816 in the garden of a German woman named Catherine Scholl, who operated a tavern and inn at Clarksburg, Maryland, near Washington, D.C. Adlum took cuttings of the vine and planted them at his one-hundred-acre experimental station in what is now Cleveland Park along Connecticut Avenue in Washington, D.C. Tested among other grapes, the Catawba became the standout. He made four hundred gallons of wine in 1822, sending one bottle to Thomas Jefferson, who was unimpressed. Undaunted, Adlum promoted his new Catawba find voraciously on the East Coast.

Longworth's first successful Catawba tenant was Anthony Tuchfarber, who purchased the lease on an unusually broken piece of ground on Bold Face Creek. He had been the third Longworth tenant on that plot, the first two being unsuccessful in fruiting any vines. Longworth tasked Tuchfarber with trenching and benching six acres of vines and planting fruit trees in three years. He was permitted to grow cabbage and potatoes and allowed a grazing area for his livestock. So, with the help of his team of healthy and grown children, to Longworth's surprise, Tuchfarber was able to fulfill his lease agreement. Longworth returned to the farm to find six acres handsomely trenched and walled-in fruit-bearing vines, as well as apple and peach trees planted. Longworth commented in an October 8, 1845 letter to the *Horticultural Review* that Tuchfarber's vineyard was one of the few left in Cincinnati that contained the Isabella grapes. To further encourage Tuchfarber and other successful growers on Bold Face Creek, Longworth offered them his share of the wine made from the grapes at a reduced rate—$0.75 per gallon for Catawba, $0.625 for the Cape and $0.50 for the Isabella. The vintage of 1845 netted Tuchfarber $1,065, a great sum for a tenant. Longworth noted that there were vineyards in Delhi more productive in 1845 than his were and that he was expanding his vineyards, seeing the great opportunity in the success of his and other growers.

GRAPES TEST-GROWN BY LONGWORTH

In 1842, Longworth said that out of about sixty varieties of native grapes he had tested, only three or four were worth cultivating. By 1858, he had

Major John Adlum, shown here circa 1794 in a portrait painted by Charles Willson Peale, introduced Longworth to the Catawba grape in the 1820s. *Courtesy of the Public Library of Cincinnati and Hamilton County.*

experimented with more than one hundred native varieties and only chose twelve as suitable to making wine: Catawba, Cape, Isabella, Bland's Madera, Ohio, Lenoir, Missouri, Norton's Seedling, Herbemont, Minor's Seedling, Mammoth Catawba and White Catawba. Of those, he focused on the Catawba, with its rich Muscadine flavor, and only commercialized the Catawba and the Isabella.

After his experiment with the Cape grape in his first vineyard, he started advertising in about 1828 for native grapes in the western and southern states. He would later offer a $500 reward for a grape more hardy than the Catawba that could make a good wine. He began correspondence with a majority of the prominent American growers. Without today's technology of microsatellite DNA using Single Satellite Repeats (SSRs), there was much confusion in the industry as to some of these native grapes. There was also no grape pedigree book or standard naming system for grapes, which made it difficult to track whether the same grape was being sold by different names. For sure, there were both uneducated and devious growers who sold grape cuttings under an incorrect name that might have been touted in the horticultural journals as promising new grapes.

In Cincinnati, there were several such arguments. Werk's Diana was thought to be the Herbemont. The Delaware was thought by many of Longworth's German tenants to be either the Traminer or the Red Riesling of Europe. The Lenoir was thought to be the same as the Herbemont. And finally, Longworth's Ohio or Cigar Box grape was thought to be the same as the Herbemont as well. Longworth himself sold several cuttings under new names that were later proven to be just seedlings of the Isabella and the Catawba.

He even experimented with foreign grapes, importing French grapes from around Paris, Bordeaux, Madeira and the Jura Mountains, but all failed to proliferate. Longworth thus declared European grapes unfit for growing in America.

The Ohio or Cigar Box grape—provided by an anonymous grower who left a cutting with Longworth's gardener—was one of the first grapes Longworth received from his 1828 advertisements requesting native grapes. It was confused with the Herbemont and created a great debate in the horticultural journals.

One of Longworth's earliest and longest grape consultants was Samuel Miller of Camden, Pennsylvania, and later Bluffton, Missouri. Longworth sent Miller some Isabella seeds that Miller later called the Louisa. Miller also cultivated the Alvey grape, which Longworth tried close to the end of his life, as it was considered a new introduction in 1860.

In 1829, Longworth wrote to William Lindsay of Washington, D.C., asking about the Cook grape, which he had heard about from Colonel Brent. Lindsay had been the gardener to the Duke of Devonshire at Chiswich House. The grape bunches of the Cook were large and shouldered and the berries small and black, with a very sweet flavor, but Longworth didn't deem them good enough to grow or use to make wine.

In 1830, Longworth wrote to Thomas S. Pleasants of Goochland County, Virginia, about the Beaverdam grape. It was reported to be a dark-purple berry, smaller, with thin skin, one to two seeds in each and a sweet, juicy and pulpy grape but without foxy flavor.

In the mid-1840s, Longworth wrote to John Bailey, who sent him Cowan grapes; J. Battery sent him McNeil grapes; and Reverend J. Wheeler of Burlington, Vermont, sent him Lyman grapes. He tested their must, which he viewed as favorable, and requested cuttings of the Lyman, which were found growing in his vineyard after his death.

In the 1830s, Mark Twain's father, James Marshall Clemens, sent grapes from his vineyard in Jamestown, Tennessee, to Longworth for review. They were probably Riverbank, Muscadine or Frost grapes that grew wild in the area. Longworth replied that they would make as good a wine as the Catawba.

In 1846, Longworth made wine from the Catawba, Cape, Isabella and Missouri. He was growing the Ohio, Catawba, Graham, Elsinboro, Clarkson's Eastern Catawba, Indiana, White Fox, Piqua, Herbemont, Giant Catawba, Minor's Seedling, Norton's Virginia Seedling, Improved Purple Fox, Missouri, Helen, Lake, Guignard and White Seedling Catawba. He dismissed the Indiana, White Fox, Piqua, Norton, Red Fox, Lake and Guignard grapes. Longworth said of the Guignard in 1842 that it is equal to the Herbemont as a table grape but does not make a good wine.

Minor's Seedling was also called the Venango and was made by the French in Fort Venango in 1803 on the Allegheny River; it had even been seen by John James Dufour in his travels in 1779. In 1856, Longworth thought that the Venango, even though its juice was not as abundant as the Catawba or Isabella, would be good to mix with and flavor other kinds of wine. It was identified as a member of the Red Fox grape family. However, others thought it to be too foxy and not suitable for wine. This is probably why Longworth never made a blend of it.

After growing the Norton by 1846 and making wine of it in 1850, Longworth discarded it, saying that it would not make a good wine. He also said that it was a bad bearer on the vine. Indeed, Norton is a smaller grape, produces less bunches and takes longer to fruit. But there is a knowledge in Europe that smaller grapes produce better wine because the flavor and sugar are concentrated. Longworth was used to the large, prolific grapes produced by the Catawba. After rejecting the Norton twice, in 1863 (the year of his death) he wrote to Hermann Missouri growers asking for new cuttings of it.

While Cincinnati growers were concerned about the volume of juice produced from the grape, the Missouri growers were more concerned about the quality and flavor of the juice than its volume. It was a known pruning procedure in Italy and other European wine growing regions to prune out excess grapes to have the fruit riper and make a richer wine. The mode of Missouri seemed to pay out for them, while Cincinnati growers pursued a quixotic quest for a grape that could produce as much as Catawba did.

Longworth also discarded the Charter Oak grape that he had been sent from Connecticut, saying of it, "The Charter Oak is all fox, of monstrous size, but its only value would be for cannon balls should the south carry division so far as to resort to bloodshed."

Longworth even corresponded on grapes with his unmarried sister, Catherine Longworth, in New Jersey. In 1853, she grew in her garden the Malaga (of which Henry Ives claimed his grape was a hybrid) and the Missouri, which Longworth noted grew better in New Jersey than Cincinnati. The Traminer was popular and proven in New Jersey, which is probably why he tried it.

Around 1860, Nicholas Longworth tried the Oporto Grape must to make wine and said of it, "Must as black as ink, and thicker than I have seen." Longworth thought it a native grape, not foreign—"if the Oporto is thoroughly hardy, I cannot think it a foreign grape."

Of all the viticulturists Longworth corresponded with, he probably respected Nicholas Herbemont (1771–1839) the most. He received the Lenoir, Herbemont and Isabella grapes from him in 1828. Herbemont was born in Jonchères, a village near Reims, France, the Champagne capital of the world. The Herbemont grape was processed into white, rosé and light red wines, while the Lenoir (also called the Black Spanish grape) was made into deep red wines. They became the foundation for southern winegrowers, while the Catawba, Norton, Ives and Delaware became the foundation for the Ohio River Valley. He corresponded with Herbemont for several years, sending him wine made from the Cape in 1830 (which Herbemont liked, although Longworth was not fond of it). Longworth had fruited the Herbemont by 1842 in many of his vineyards and named one of the roads in his Bald Hill vineyards Herbemont in his honor.

Longworth said of the Isabella:

> In all my early vineyards, I cultivated the Isabella extensively. I cultivated it on the tops and sides of hills, with all exposures and on bottoms. I have cultivated it for twenty five years and still have a few of them in three of my vineyards, and a few in my garden. It is the worst grape for ripening we have. Usually half the berries continue green, and they are also liable to rot. My German vine-dressers have extirpated it from their vineyards, or are now doing it. It is best manufactured into a sweet wine, by adding one and a half, or two pounds of white Havana sugar to the gallon.

In a letter to Longworth in 1829, Herbemont posed a question that would influence Longworth's path: "Why not be satisfied with any good wine, sui generis, which the country, soil and climate permit to make, and which though different, may be of equal value or perhaps superior to the imported ones?" Even though Longworth got the Catawba from Major Adlum, he continued to plant it with the guidelines in his several letters exchanged with Herbemont. He also used Herbemont's recommendation to not use sugar and brandy to fortify his wines and to never call his sparkling wines Champagne. Herbemont recommended high trellises, maximizing air circulation to avoid rot, different from what they did in Europe, and deep trenching for the roots.

The Herbemont growing ended for the most part in the 1870s, when the phylloxera outbreak in France caused nearly every Herbemont planting in North America to be uprooted and shipped overseas to provide resistant rootstocks to graft their European *vinifera* onto. Because it did not grow easily from cuttings and rejected grafts, it would be replaced by other American native rootstocks in the 1880s.

In 1850, Longworth sent to Boston for bunches of the Diana grape to compare to the Catawba. It is significant for being a female cultivated grape, like the original Catawba, having been hybridized by Mrs. Diana Ames Crehore of Milton, Massachusetts. After sampling, he deemed it much inferior to the Catawba—with a harder pulp, more seeds and a foxier flavor—and so not worth growing. The provider from Boston, Mr. Downing, warned him that in order for it to be truly tested, it must be grown and allowed to fully ripen in Cincinnati.

Longworth received the Delaware grape in 1849 from George Campbell of Delaware, Ohio. In 1860, he said in a letter to George Ellwanger of Rochester, New York, that a sample of wine from the Delaware was the best wine he ever made; it possessed more body and was a heaver wine. Other Cincinnati growers like Mottier and Bogen also grew Delaware and made wines. Delaware wine was on the menus of such resorts as the Chester Park clubhouse, and it made it into a grape-flavored soft drink called Delaware Punch that is now owned by Coca-Cola.

In 1853, Longworth hosted at his mansion the first tasting of wines using the 100 point rating system that is used today to judge wine. At that tasting, he offered wines he had made from three new grapes—Cox, Danville and Winter.

Although Longworth grew the Delaware and Norton, two grapes more resistant than the Catawba that also made good wines, he never grew or made wine of the Ives, the grape that took off among growers on the East Side of Cincinnati in the 1860s, after his death. He also never grew the Concord, which became the American dominant grape for wines and, later, jellies, juice and flavorings.

He would never award the $500 to a grower with a grape hardier than the Catawba. And he never found a red grape suitable for commercialization. He did shower praise and awards on local Catawba growers like Rentz,

Mottier, Heckinger and his beloved tenant Christian Schniecke. But he scoffed at the most obvious red grape choice, the Norton, which grew well in Hamilton County, saying that it did not make a suitable wine. The Missouri Germans latched onto the Norton grape and built a wonderful wine industry that still makes Norton wines today. Longworth died a bit too early for the Ives grape, which also grew well and was first cultivated in Cincinnati. The Longworth Wine House made Ives wine from grapes grown in Plainville in 1869, six years after Longworth's death and the year his descendants sold the wine house.

Longworth's mission in getting into wine was threefold. He saw wine as a temperance beverage—one that would wipe out the evils of whiskey. Cincinnati was a huge whiskey town before it was a Catawba and beer town. He saw how whiskey ruined the poor families who rented his many properties in Cincinnati and wanted to put a stop to it. He cited reports from wine country in Europe stating that the problems of alcoholism were not present there and that health in wine country exceeded that of those outside its boundaries. While not a teetotaler, Longworth would have been happy to see whiskey phased out of existence. Second, he wanted to lift people up economically by giving them good employment in a good industry. He was known for his charity and his soft spot for those in need. He was responsible for the arrival of thousands of Germanic immigrants at the height of the Catawba Craze. Thirdly, he wanted to create a sustainable and native grape wine industry that could grow and compete against European wines being imported, one that we could be proud of.

Longworth achieved all three, although creating a sustainable wine industry for Cincinnati was short-lived. Longworth played his role in passing the torch of the American wine industry. We weren't the first location, but we accepted the torch from the Swiss of Vevay, Indiana. Longworth then inadvertently passed the torch along to Lake Erie, Missouri, and New York, which then in turn passed the torch on to California before Prohibition.

The thousands of immigrants whom Longworth actively sponsored to work in the wine industry made significant impacts on the cultural and economic development of the city of Cincinnati. Longworth's go-to market using immigrant tenants on land he owned reduced his expenses in labor and created the supply of good grapes for winemaking. And while this tenant economy was more advantageous to him, he did provide a portal for the immigrants who built our city. He funded the research and made recommendations, but his tenants were ultimately responsible for the success of their vineyards.

Longworth became a guerrilla marketer of Catawba wine. He solicited big names for endorsement like King Wilhelm I of Baden-Wuertemburg and poets like William Wadsworth Longfellow, who created the famous poem about Catawba wine, giving our city the nickname "Queen City of the West." While Longworth did not have the dash of Dr. John Aston Warder, the science of Louis Rehfuss or the sex appeal of Longfellow, people listened to or read what Longworth had to say in the horticultural journals of the time, which was like social media for the wine industry.

Tiny Bubbles Make a Sparkling Market in Cincinnati

The production of sparkling wines in Cincinnati started in the early 1840s on a small scale. A Frenchman, Valentine Miller (1807–1876), was the first to produce them. His vineyard, wine house and wine garden were in Westwood, next to that of Michael Werk, to whom he also taught the craft. Miller also worked with the Bogen brothers of Carthage to make their first Sparkling Catawba in 1847. The next year, together they made forty thousand bottles of Sparkling Catawba. Valentine Miller was proprietor of a wine garden at his farm on Harrison Pike into the 1870s. It was one of a number of wine houses flourishing on Harrison Pike—the others being those of George Fein and Michael Werk. Longworth heard of these activities and visited the operations of Miller after a happy accident occurred in his wine house.

Longworth, without intent, produced in 1842 a Sparkling Catawba. Not knowing the process but seeing its huge potential, Longworth decided that a sparkling wine would be his way to broaden the Cincinnati wine market beyond the Germanic *weinstuben* and coffee houses. After trying and failing to duplicate his first accidental success, he sent for a Frenchman in 1845. Unfortunately, that man drowned in the Ohio before using his secrets at the Longworth Wine House. It took Longworth two more years to find a successor, who began making the bubbles in 1847, the same year as the Bogens's first release. The man was born in Reims and was living in New York before being recruited to Cincinnati. Although the winemaker was French, Longworth was quite firm about his vision to produce a sparkling wine from native grapes. "I shall not attempt to imitate any of the sparkling wines of Europe," he wrote in 1849; instead, he aimed to provide "a pure article having the peculiar flavor of our native grape."

Regarding his making Sparkling Catawba:

For two years past [1844] *I have tried the manufacture of "Champagne" wine on a small scale. The result convinces me that we can rival the best imported. I have obtained an experienced manufacturer from France, and am now digging a vault and erecting a house, to have it manufactured on a large scale; impending, as soon as the character of the wine is established, and its successful manufacture proven, to transfer the business to other hands.*

In 1845, Longworth wrote about Sparkling Catawba:

I have long thought that Catawba wine, under proper management, would make either a good sparkling Hock or Champagne. The experiment has recently been tried with success by Mr. T.H. Miller [Valentine Miller], *who has prepared some specimens of Champagne from the Catawba wine of last year. In company with two of our most eminent wine merchants, I lately called on Mr. Miller, and compared the American Champagne with the French. They concurred with me in the opinion that under proper management, a first rate article of Champagne can be made from the Catawba wine, and sold at a fair price.*

With the help of Joe Siefert, a building contractor and later Ives winemaker, Longworth in 1846 built a forty-by-fifty-foot cellar specifically for Sparkling Catawba. In 1848, he made six thousand bottles; in 1849, he produced ten thousand bottles; and by 1850, he was turning out sixty thousand bottles per year and had plans for national distribution of his wine. This he began in 1852, by which time he had two cellars dedicated to sparkling wine and oversaw a production of about seventy-five thousand bottles.

The wine was made by the traditional *méthode champenoise*, in which after a dose of sugar was added to the wine following its first fermentation, a second fermentation was carried out in the bottles and the resulting sediment cleared. Since it was ripened in the bottle, Sparkling Catawba required fifteen to twenty months for maturing before it was ready to be sold.

Losses from bursting bottles were expected to be about 5 to 10 percent. Longworth had gutters in his wine cellars to collect this loss, which would be distilled into Catawba brandy. If there was no loss at all, the fermentation would be questioned. The second French immigrant Longworth hired had been a few years in New York City, resuscitating imported Champagnes for the importing houses. Longworth was skeptical of his skills, and sure enough, he had forty-two to fifty thousand bottles burst under the pressure of fermentation. That manager was let go. Before specific gravity and sugar content was understood, it was kind of a guessing game to the wine manager as to how much sugar should be added to the second fermentation.

Jacques Fournier arrived from Reims, France, in 1851 and applied more science and skill than his predecessors. In 1858, Fournier's salary was noted as $2,500 annually, with free rent and a reference to other perks. The troubles and losses of the first years were rewarded; if Americans had been put off by the foxy, dry taste of still Catawba, they were quick to enjoy a bubbly Catawba. Suddenly, Cincinnati's winegrowers, and Longworth in particular, had a national winner, a widely advertised and widely enjoyed proof that the United States could produce an acceptable wine.

By 1851, there was a market for Sparkling Catawba and sparkling native grape wines in Cincinnati. The Bogens produced thirty-five thousand bottles in 1851 and twenty-six thousand in 1850. Corneau and Sons produced ten thousand bottles of both still and Sparkling Catawba. And our "Cincinnati Champagne" wasn't limited to Catawba. Werk made sparkling Norton, Ives, Delaware, Catawba and Isabella. Christian Schniecke made a sparkling Herbemont with the help of Fournier.

In 1852, Cincinnati commercial bottlers together produced 245,000 bottles of sparkling wine. Two years later, Longworth reported making 200,000 bottles of Sparkling Catawba himself. The commercial makers of sparkling wine were Werk, Longworth, Bogen, Corneau, Yeatman and Miller. Longworth gave reason for his entrée into the sparkling wine market, saying that making still wine into sparkling wine doubled its market price.

In 1852, the Ohio Agricultural Society gave Longworth the silver cup for his Sparkling Catawba. At the New York World's Fair in Bryant Park in 1854, Longworth's Sparkling Isabella won the prize for best wine in America. The sparkling wines brought the market out of the Germanic coffee houses and into prominent venues like the Gibson House, which served in 1856 Sparkling Catawba wines from Longworth, Bogen and J.D. Park of Covington, Kentucky. In 1857, Longworth's Sparkling Catawba was on the menu at the Golden Lamb Hotel, then called the Lebanon House.

After 1858, Longworth branded his premium Sparkling Catawba "Golden Wedding" after his fiftieth anniversary, celebrated with Susan Howell Longworth on Christmas Eve 1857. This was made from premium grapes chosen from Cincinnati vineyards.

The next French Champagne experts to arrive at the Longworth Wine House were cousins Jules (1833–1920) and Joseph Masson (1829–1872). Jules Masson was born in the tiny village of Marnoz, France, in the Burgundy wine country. Louis Pasteur lived in Marnoz in his early life, and his first experiments with pasteurization were with wine. Masson was summoned by Longworth, or perhaps Fournier, to make his Sparkling Catawba. Jules and Joseph landed in New Orleans and took a steamboat up the Mississippi to the Ohio, landing in Cincinnati and at Longworth's wine house in 1852. The cousins married sisters Catherine and Apollonia Rheinhardt from Niederkirchen, Germany.

Although there's no record of it, it would make sense that Jules Masson apprenticed and learned the art of winemaking at Courvoisier (the winery, not the brandy folks), also in Marnoz, his home village. It would have made a great résumé for Longworth to have seen to agree to their employment. The likelihood is strengthened by the fact that there was intermarriage between the Masson and Courvoisier families in 1770, according to village records.

In 1869, when the Longworth Wine House was sold, the Masson families moved to Hammandsport, New York, to work for a new winery that had been started there. Hammondsport, much like Cincinnati, sits in a long, narrow, beautiful valley whose hills are dotted with vineyards, pastures and woodlands. It sits on the southern tip of Lake Keuka in what is known today as the Finger Lakes region. Jules became works manager and champagne maker for the Pleasant Valley Wine Company, which was formed in 1860 by Charles D. Champlin and several others. It made a pure white altar wine in 1883 that the Cincinnati Archdiocese used.

Jules and Joseph were intimately familiar with both the Catawba and Isabella grapes, as well as other native varieties that Longworth had grown. Jules took over as works manager and winemaker in 1869 for the wine company. Joseph become a prominent vineyardist in Hammondsport. His vineyards began on a hilltop overlooking Lake Keuka five miles north of Hammondsport and extended to the lake itself.

Three of Jules's sons worked at various times at the winery: Arthur, who died young; Leon; and Victor. Victor studied chemical engineering at Lehigh University and as a winemaker put the fermentation process, until then somewhat haphazard, into some scientific regularity. He was known for a very sweet, Tokay-like dessert wine he made before Prohibition. Victor later became a consultant to several American wineries, including Cooks.

Champlin's idea was to improve on Longworth's wines using the same French Champagne method. The first successful sparkling vintage came in 1870 with a blend of Catawba and Delaware grapes. The Massons knew the sparkling Delaware wines made by Bogen and Werk in Cincinnati. In 1871, some of these new champagnes were taken to the Parker House Hotel in

Right: An advertisement for what Longworth and Zimmerman branded a "ladies' wine" made from the Isabella grape. *Courtesy of the Public Library of Cincinnati and Hamilton County.*

Below: A family portrait of Jules Masson, former sparkling wine manager for Longworth, who went on to own Pleasant Valley Winery in Hammondsport, New York. *Courtesy of Champlin family.*

Boston for judging at a great dinner party. Among the prestigious guests was Marshall Wilder, a friend of Champlin's and a prominent horticulturist, who proclaimed that the Pleasant Valley wine was a great sparkling wine from the new western world—the name Great Western was born. The brand lives on as a trademark of the Pleasant Valley Wine Company.

The winery received great publicity at the 1873 Vienna Exposition, where the Great Western champagne won first prize. This triumph, along with top honors in Brussels and Paris, allowed Pleasant Valley to market its sparkling wine as award winning for the next hundred years. Masson's Great Western champagne competed at the Vienna Exposition against those of his Cincinnati winemaking colleagues: Werk's Golden Eagle Sparkling Catawba, Bogen's Diamond Sparkling Catawba and E.A. Thompson's Hillside Sparkling Catawba. The blend of Catawba and Delaware grapes of the Great Western champagne distinguished its unique taste and put Hammondsport, New York, on the map.

With the Massons' expertise blazing the trail, others followed suit, and by the end of the nineteenth century, more than fifty wineries around the Finger Lakes were producing bubbles on a grand scale, thanks to the brilliance of Jules Masson, Longworth's former sparkling winemaker. At one point, historians estimate that more than 7 million bottles were being sold annually, with an astonishing 90 percent of all American sparkling wine coming out the Hammondsport area.

LONGWORTH'S BRANDY AND BITTERS

By 1850, Longworth had a growing sparkling wine business in addition to his still wines. The last piece of the puzzle was Catawba brandy and bitters. He saw a market for medicinal Catawba wine bitters, which required good Catawba brandy. His fellow winemakers like John Corneau across the river in Latonia, Kentucky, were selling it widely. But Longworth didn't own a still or have experience in distillation. He needed an experienced partner who also had a laboratory so he could obtain a respected medicinal reference. He saw that in the Zimmermans, a Baden immigrant family who had a factory with cellars and wine distribution center at 177 Sycamore Street. Their chemical laboratory, the most important piece, was located at Sixth Street between Freeman and Canal.

So, Longworth put up $65,000 in 1851 to partner with Caspar Zimmerman (1828–1881) and his brothers Anton, John and Phillip. The Zimmermans were good chemists, something Longworth was not. They particularly understood the stoichiometry and ratios of chemicals needed for making brandy and bitters. Longworth relied on his winemakers for the methods. Longworth was looking for a way to use sparkling wine that had burst the bottles. He had special channels installed in his wine house to collect this waste. He could recoup some of this loss by distilling it into brandy and then making some of it into bitters.

John Zimmerman was the leading chemist of the brothers and wrote about the medicinal benefits of well-made Catawba brandy in medical journals. Catawba brandy was made from the skins and the sediment of the grape, also called lees, produced during fermentation. He pointed out that there were a lot of fake brandies on the market, made from diluted corn alcohol, with flavoring of grape pumice and coloring. These could be easily detected by isolating the corn-fusel oil.

Zimmerman, with help from Longworth, began making Sparkling Catawba. In 1852, Zimmerman bottled 30,000 bottles; in 1853, 50,000; in 1854, 75,000; and in 1855, 100,000. This speaks to the increasing yield of grape crops locally from 1848 to 1851, most of which probably came from Longworth's vineyards.

The Longworth-Zimmerman partnership only lasted until about 1854. Longworth withdrew and took wine in casks, brandy and one half of the sparkling wine in payment, with the name of Longworth and Zimmerman put on the labels. But the Zimmermans used Longworth's name for several years after the dissolution of the partnership, and Longworth continued to make Catawba bitters and brandy until 1863. Longworth's Catawba bitters was sold as being made from pure Catawba brandy and warranted to cure the worst cases of dysentery and diarrhea. The ads many times were directed at Civil War soldiers as a remedy for change of climate and fatigue.

In 1852, Longworth's biggest wine competitors locally were Robert Buchanan, Corneau & Sons in Latonia, George and Peter Bogen, Rehfuss, Thomas Yeatman, Valentin Miller and a few others. All labeled their wines for sale regionally and nationally. Their aggregate production in 1852 was 150,000 bottles of still wine and 180,000 bottles of sparkling wine—of which volume Longworth made about 60 percent.

Another estimated thirty thousand bottles of still Catawba wine was made, sold and drank locally by Germans at the hundreds of coffee houses in the German quarters of Cincinnati and Northern Kentucky. This was all unbranded wine, mostly the product of small vineyards on the West Side or the few on the East Side. In 1852, the height of the Catawba Craze, there were 1,200 acres of grapes cultivated in Greater Cincinnati. Each year, more and more vines came into bearing, as it took between four and seven years for newly planted vines to produce. The success drove more to get into the business to reap the profits. In 1852, demand was so strong for native Catawba wines that all wines older than five years were out of the market. Sparkling wine, although only requiring half of the aging as still Catawba, was taken off as fast as could be made.

An advertisement for Longworth Catawba bitters touts its ability to cure diarrhea. *Courtesy of the Public Library of Cincinnati and Hamilton County.*

This lower class of wine was cheaper than Longworth's and the other branded wines and was of various but mostly inferior quality. There was no Two Buck Chuck version of Longworth's wines. With all his money invested in advertising, he was shooting for the higher end of the market, and most Cincinnati middle-class Germans may have never been able to afford to taste his wine. Longworth wines would not have been served consistently at the corner coffee house in Over-the-Rhine, but rather at the high-end hotels like the Gibson House or the St. Nicholas Hotel. The owner of the St. Nicholas, Balthasar Roth, a Rhineland immigrant, bought out the remaining inventory of the Longworth Wine House when it closed in 1869 and served it for many years.

An 1867 review by German immigrant travel writer Friedrich Gerstacker of Catawba wine being made by the Longworth Wine House gives us an interesting perspective. He noted during his visit to Cincinnati in 1867, three years after Longworth's death, that "[t]he owners [of Longworth Wine House] maintain some important vineyards, and on four or five of them raise various Catawba grapes. With the exception of one, however, a lovely strong wine, the Catawba has too much tartness for me, and reminds me of Meissner's wine, and that is the best that can be said of it. One wine was exceptional, a so-called Ives Seedling rosé wine with a pleasant and light strawberry taste to it." Meissner wines came from the town of Meissen, northwest of Dresden in the kingdom of Saxony in the northernmost winemaking region of Germany. Gerstacker worked in Saxony and would have been familiar with this type of wine, made from regional white grapes. The Ives Seedling was a Cincinnati-originated varietal just getting traction with East Side growers in and around the village of Madeira.

By the end of it all, Longworth had three clusters of vineyards totaling 122 acres. He had Bold Face Creek in Delhi (1823), the Garden of Eden in Mount Adams (1844) and Bald Face Hill (1840s) in Columbia-Tusculum. He had two wine cellars—and the interest in a third with the Zimmermans for about five years. He commercially produced still and Sparkling Catawba and Isabella wines, Catawba brandy and Catawba bitters. He tested more than one hundred native varieties of grapes and made only about twenty-five types of wine in small batches. He had sent wine to Germany, England, Italy and across the United States. He had created an international notoriety for Cincinnati Catawba wine. He employed about twenty men at a time in his main wine house and sponsored hundreds of immigrants as tenants in his vineyards. They and their descendants built the character of Cincinnati.

LONGWORTH'S
TWO BEST VINEYARDISTS

Longworth frequently complained about his stubborn "Swoabs" who would not bend from the traditional viticulture methods of their fatherland. "Swoab" was a derogatory term associated with provincial close-mindedness and used to describe the Swabian Germans from the kingdom of Baden-Wuertemburg. The irony was that he had recruited and hired them because of their experience but quickly found that they needed to be more open to methods that were favorable to the native grapes and unique climate of America. Even more ironic is that his two best vineyardists were not from the Rhine Rhombus—the fifty-mile radius in the southwest Germanic kingdom of Baden-Wuertemburg from which he had recruited tenants. They were from Switzerland and Saxony, both outside of wine country. John E. Mottier was the shining star out of Longworth's Bold Face Creek vineyards on the West Side, and Christian Schniecke was the leading vineyardist in his Garden of Eden vineyard.

John E. Mottier: Tracing Early American Wine

Longworth started his commercial wine enterprise in Delhi at his Bold Face Creek vineyards. His first tenants were Anthony Tuchfarber and Johann P. Amman. But another early tenant of those vineyards tells the larger tale of the migration of American wine from East Coast to West Coast. That *vigneron* was John E. Mottier, a Swiss immigrant. Mottier's story spans the trajectory

John Emmanuel Mottier, a Swiss immigrant, was one of Longworth's first tenants and one of his most successful winegrowers, operating from his farm in Delhi. *Courtesy of North East Pennsylvania Historical Society.*

of Cincinnati and American wine. Mottier's vineyard was one of the earliest and largest vineyards in Cincinnati. He is connected through his wife's family to the Dufours in the Swiss immigrant colony in Vevay, Indiana, who started the cultivation of the Cape or Alexander grape. Mottier's tale then extends to Lake Erie growers, who along with the Germanic vineyardists of Hermann, Missouri, took on the torch from Cincinnati. His family would unite with Longworth's other most successful vineyardist, Christian Schniecke, with the marriage of his daughter Maria Mottier and Friedrich Schniecke. Through Mottier, the American wine torch would be passed from Philadelphia to Lexington, Kentucky; to Vevay, Indiana; to Cincinnati; and then to Lake Erie shore. He brought his experience with the Cape grape to Longworth's land and then learned the Catawba at Longworth's urging, as well as the Delaware, taking that experience to the South Shore Winery in Pennsylvania.

John Emmanuel Mottier (1801–1887) was born on August 9 in Ormont-Dessus, Canton Vaud, Switzerland. He was the eldest of three sons of John E. and Maria T. (Favre) Mottier, both natives of Switzerland, of French ancestry. Canton Vaud has a winemaking tradition that dates back to the Middle Ages, with vineyards cultivated by Cistercian monks. Today, it is the second-biggest wine producing region of Switzerland, with the white grape Chasselas being the most common grape grown. It produces a wine with a variety of fruity, floral and mineral flavors, as well as with good acidity and the ability to age well in the cellar.

At the time of Mottier's birth, the American wine industry was just getting its legs. John James Dufour (1763–1827) would start the ball rolling in the American wine industry and would become Mottier's uncle-in-law. Dufour would become the first American winegrower to succeed in making wine in commercial quantities. He latched onto the Cape or Alexander grape like Longworth did the Catawba. Dufour and Longworth even had a lifelong feud over which grape was the best grape—the nonnative Cape or the native Catawba. Dufour had come to America from Switzerland in 1796. After experimenting with a vineyard near Lexington, Kentucky, he petitioned the U.S. government for a deferred grant to purchase lands and start a wine colony in Vevay, Indiana.

Longworth remarked that it was the method of the Swiss to ferment the wine with the skins that made a bad wine with native grapes because it increased the wine's foxiness—a flavor that was new and unlikeable to most European wine drinkers. As to the quality of the wine of Vevay, opinions varied according to the experience and loyalties of the critic. Those who liked it compared it to the best Bordeaux claret; those who didn't were quite derogatory.

Mottier immigrated to America at age eighteen, arriving at New York on July 5, 1821. He was listed as a domestic with the David Pernet family, who also settled near Vevay. He worked for them for three years in a sort of indentured servant arrangement, known as a "redemptionist," to pay his passage across the Atlantic. After his labor had paid for his passage, he began working as a farmhand, which he did for three more years. In July 1827, he married Mary, one of the three Siebenthal sisters. Mary was daughter of Jean François Siebenthal and Jeanne Marie Dufour, part of the original Swiss wine colony at Vevay.

With his new wife, John moved to Delhi in 1829 in Hamilton County, Ohio. They were one of several families recruited by Nicholas Longworth when he visited Vevay, Indiana. Fredrick Diserens, who owned the William Tell Exchange in downtown Cincinnati in the 1840s and 1850s, was an original member of the Vevay colony, and his was probably another family recruited by Longworth. He was also a member of the American Winegrowers' Association. Diserens grew and made wine from Herbemont, Catawba and Isabella grapes in the 1860s.

Another family from the Vevay colony who came to Cincinnati was that of Henry Brachman and his wife, Rosalia Bettens. While Henry was from Nordhausen, Prussia, his wife was born in Vevay, Indiana, to Phillip and Rosalia Bettens, members of the original seventeen Swiss immigrant families. Brachman owned a ninety-nine-acre farm with a Catawba vineyard that spanned both sides of Beechmont Avenue between Beacon Street and Burney Lane. Their farmhouse sat on Brachman Street.

By the 1840s, John Mottier had made quite a name for himself, and his vineyard and grapes were well known. An article in the October 1840 *Western Farmer* detailed a visit to his vineyard:

> *On Wednesday the 16th rode down with a small party to a vineyard owned by Longworth but leased by Mottier who is his own vigneron. It is kept in fine order everything neat and business like. There are about seven acres*

planted, only about 2/3 of which however is yet in bearing. The varieties found to suit best are the Catawba, Isabella and Black Cape.

After Mottier started his first vineyard in 1829, the vines started fruiting in two and three years, and for the next fifteen years, he only lost one crop from the effects of frost, drought or any other cause. He liked a northern exposure over a southern, as the vines on the latter sometimes suffered partially from spring frosts but never on a northern.

In 1844, Mottier made about 1,500 gallons of wine, which he sold at one dollar per gallon. His Catawba white wine was compared to Rhine wine; his Cape red wine was compared to a Burgundy. He consistently yielded 200 to 400 gallons of wine per acre.

In 1845, after more than fifteen years as a Longworth tenant, John Mottier struck out on his own and bought his own property, which now encompasses the Dunham recreation center on Guerley Avenue and the former Dunham Tuberculosis Hospital. He even branded his own wine, National Premium Catawba.

Mottier sponsored two of his brothers to immigrate to Cincinnati. The first was John D. in 1846, and then Abraham E. came over in 1850 with his wife and seven children. John D. would end up in Patriot, Indiana, crop raising and stock farming, while Abraham would settle in Moscow, Ohio, among other Brown County winegrowers.

An 1850s wine label from John Mottier's National Premium Catawba Wine, made in Delhi. *Courtesy of the North East Pennsylvania Historical Society.*

During the Civil War, Mottier lent two of his sons and vineyard workers to the Union cause: Favor Z., who served in the Fiftieth Ohio, Company H, and who was held for six months as a prisoner at Andersonville; and Charles Helvetius, a member of the Fourth Ohio Cavalry. Favor paid the ultimate price when he died in 1867 of complications due to his service.

In 1867, Dr. John Aston Warder described the secret to Mottier's success in growing grapes—his method of preventing the odium or vine black rot. Mottier used air-slaked lime in combination with sulfur. To a portion of his vines, he applied the lime alone and, as he thought, with equally good effect. Although still being disputed, it was believed (and later proved) that odium or black rot was brought on by microscopic insects called phylloxera. Many vineyardists in Europe and America argued that sulfur alone adhered to the grapes and gave them an off flavor that made them unsellable and unfavorable for wine.

One of the last things Mottier did before leaving Cincinnati was to defend that it was a good grape growing region, despite Thomas Yeatman's letter to the contrary to the Cincinnati Horticultural Society in 1864. Mottier planted 1,200 Delaware vines in 1860 and 2,000 more in 1861. At a Cincinnati Horticultural Society meeting, Mottier staged a blind tasting of his Delaware wine alongside a Johannisburg. Mottier's young Delaware scored significantly higher than the well-known Johannisburg. He sold his entire vintage of three hundred gallons of Delaware wine that year for six dollars per gallon.

In 1865, Mottier was offered a job he couldn't refuse. Colonel J. Condit Smith, a retired army colonel and the president of the South Shore Wine Company in North East, Pennsylvania, offered him the chief winemaker job. Smith had heard about Mottier's winemaking prowess after he had been appointed the chairman of the National Committee for Grapes by the Cincinnati Horticultural Society. Smith offered to pay Mottier 125 shares of the capital stock of the company at the rate of 25 shares per year for five years. He was to start that year in time to make that year's harvest of grapes into wine. If Mottier wasn't able to complete the terms of the contract, his youngest son, Charles Mottier, was to do so. Both John and Charles signed the agreement. While they would be making wine with the Catawba and Delaware, they would also be using the Concord grape, which had been planted on several thousand acres in the area.

In 1870, John and Charles decided not to renew their contract with the South Shore Winery, but they still retained their stock ownership. They started their own winery, the John E. Mottier Winery, in North East,

Pennsylvania (after John's death, his son renamed it the Chestnut Grove Wine Cellar). They also started a wine basket company, turning out millions per year. They continued to cultivate the Catawba, from which they had great success in Cincinnati and grew Delaware, Ives, Norton and Wilder (Roger's #4), Isarella and Mottled varietals. They were both influential members of the Lake Shore Grape Growers Association and continued to have correspondence with their former Cincinnati wine growing friends.

John Mottier died in Dayton, Ohio, while visiting his wife's Siebenthal family and was buried in a family plot at Spring Grove Cemetery. This plot is graced with an obelisk decorated with a grape wreath and is a memorial to the early American winemaking families Dufour, Siebenthal, Mottier and Schniecke.

Longworth's Vineyardists of the Garden of Eden

Longworth had hired Daniel McAvoy to lay out the Garden of Eden vineyards in 1844 in what is now Cincinnati's Eden Park. Several families lived on and tended these vineyards. The Cash family lived in the valley close to the north basin of the reservoir and had a large vineyard. The Youngers lived at a point on the hill above the pump house near the Krohn Conservatory. The Metzgers were nearer to Deer Creek Road and west of the main carriage entrance to the park. The Heibels lived on the hill at the north end of the little viaduct and the Schnieckes on the same level, near Morris Street.

Of all these vineyardists, it was Christian Friedrich Gottlieb Schniecke (1794–1879) who was Longworth's most prolific and favorite vine dresser. It was his house and vineyard that both Longworth and his son-in-law William Flagg sent visitors to if they wanted to see a good vineyard. Schniecke managed a total of twelve acres of vineyards for Longworth and lived there with his wife; daughter, Amelia (1825–1863); and three sons, Friedrich (1824–1880), Moritz (1834–1867) and Henry (1838–1924). His total plot was eighteen acres, so he had about six acres for his residence and orchards and his own gardens. Schniecke even had a strawberry varietal he cultivated there called the Schniecke Prolific, which was distributed in the eastern United States before the Civil War.

Longworth said of Schniecke in 1851:

All my tenants but one, are old vineyard men. He is a worker, and a man of strong common sense, close observation, and unusual neatness. His vineyard

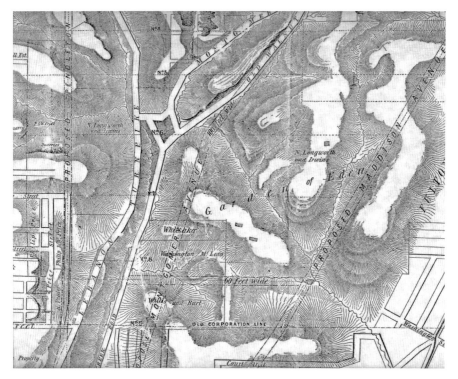

A map of Longworth's Garden of Eden vineyards. *Courtesy of the Public Library of Cincinnati and Hamilton County.*

is a pattern for all vine dressers, and his wine of superior quality. His wine of last vintage he sold from 75 cents to $1 per bottle. I myself bought of him at that price. His must weighed 96. He began making wine last year [1850], *early in October, and finished about the 24th, being from two weeks to a month later than most others.*

Schniecke was born in the north Germanic kingdom of Saxony, not in wine country. He married Sophia Wegner in Berlin in 1823 and had his four children before heading to America. They came to Cincinnati in 1838, landing as one of the first tenants of the Garden of Eden. All three of Christian's sons worked in the Garden of Eden vineyard with their father. He first started growing grapes in 1845 and got first fruit in 1847. By 1858, he had seven acres in bearing, with five more coming on. Not having a press, he made his own and won first prize for the wine made from it from the Cincinnati Horticultural Society, of which he was very proud. Schniecke's best crop was in 1850, when he pressed out 2,200 gallons from three acres.

His son Friedrich Augustus "Gus" (1824–circa 1885) married Maria Mottier, the daughter of John Mottier, who dressed Longworth's small vineyard in Delhi. But tragedy struck, as several of their children died in infancy and Maria would die in childbirth right before the Civil War. To escape the reminders of this tragedy, Friedrich left Cincinnati and within a year remarried a woman in Flint Gap, Tennessee, along the French Broad River Valley, where he started orchards and a fruit nursery business. Friedrich's son Thomas Schniecke would become a national expert on the cultivation of Japanese persimmons.

Although he grew the Catawba for Longworth and had been using it many years for wine, Schniecke ranked it last in the lineup of native grapes. He said in 1862, "I can give you my opinion of the Delaware grape in one word. It is the best kind, not of American only, but of the world. Next to Delaware I place Lincoln, then Lenoir, next Herbemont, and then perhaps Catawba. But I think Diana when it becomes more plenty may stand by Delaware."

Schniecke went on to say this about the wine made from native grapes:

> *The Delaware wine in my opinion far exceeds any native wine. It has more strength than any of the rest, and will consequently keep longer. The Lincoln wine is red and in my opinion equal to the Norton's Virginia if not superior. The Herbemont is a grape of which the qualities and advantages are not yet known, although it has been cultivated a long time. The Marion grape will produce more and make better wine than any of the Isabella species of which there are at least half a dozen kinds.*

Schniecke was quite a prolific winemaker, starting with Catawba in 1850. He made still and Sparkling Catawba, as well as wine from Minor's Seedling, the Cape and Isabella in 1858. In 1859, he made a sparkling Herbemont with Fournier, Longworth's sparkling wine manager. The year 1860 was a particularly busy one for winemaking. That year, he made wines from the Venango, a Venango/Herbemont blend, Union Village, Delaware and what he called a nice "ladies' wine" from a new Virginia Seedling, or the Norton. It even appears that he tried to brand his wine, as he made a wine that year he called Abe Lincoln's Wine from unspecified grapes.

His third son, Moritz H. Schniecke (1834–1867), was a private in Unit A of the Ohio 106th Regiment in the Civil War, also known as the 4th German unit, led by Gustav Tafel, president of the Cincinnati Turners and later mayor of Cincinnati. Moritz was discharged with disability at Franklin,

Kentucky, on March 29, 1863. He may have been wounded at the Battle of Hartsville, where the whole unit was captured. Moritz Schniecke died on March 18, 1867.

In 1859, Charles Mackay described a visit to Schniecke's vineyard:

> *Mr. Longworth's son-in-law* [William Flagg] *kindly gave our party an invitation to accompany him on a visit to the vineyards. They are situated on a hilltop and slope overlooking the windings of the beautiful Ohio. We there found an old soldier of Napoleon, from Saxe-Weimar, who fought at Waterloo, and afterwards retired to his native fields to cultivate the vine. Mr. Longworth having sent to Europe for persons skilled in the manufacture of the Rheinish wines, had the fortune to discover this excellent old man, good soldier and skillful vintage. Soon after his arrival he was placed in the responsible position of chief wine maker and superintendent under Mr. Longworth, and here, like Bacchus of old times he teaches people how to plant, and tend and press the vine, and use for health and strength and length of days the treasure of the rich full bodied grape....We ended by repairing to his domicile on the crown of the hill where he set before us bread and cheese, and a whole constellation of wines.*

After the Longworth Wine House was sold, Schniecke bought a home at 589 Sycamore Street, where he spent the rest of his years with his wife. Although there's no portrait of Schniecke known to exist, it's believed that he is represented in the lower-left corner of the standing portrait of Nicholas Longworth produced by Robert Duncanson in 1858, now hanging in the Taft Museum. In it we see a vineyard worker in broad-brimmed straw hat, pantaloons and work shirt coming toward the house, possibly to pick up a group from Longworth's mansion to lead to his vineyard.

THE CATAWBA CRAZE
AND ITS BARONS

Longworth's success and wide promotion of the local wine industry inspired other wealthy capitalists to take up winemaking. This began Cincinnati's Catawba Craze, which lasted about twenty-five years from 1840 to the end of the Civil War in 1865. His quote in the September 1, 1847 *Prairie Farmer* is the seminal phrase that got things started: "The day is not too distant when the banks of the Ohio will rival the banks of the Rhine, in the quality and quantity of wine produced. Our German emigrants are the people who will accomplish it." As it turns out, many would follow a rich Yankee's advice.

On February 14, 1842, at the home of Robert Buchanan on Fourth Street, several of the largest growers founded the Cincinnati Horticultural Society. It was formed for the purpose of exchanging information on cultivation of ornamental and edible fruits, vegetables, flowers, trees and shrubs. The society hosted spring and fall exhibitions well attended by out-of-towners and published regular reports on the culture of the grape. The minutes of its weekly meetings were reported in the *Cincinnati Enquirer*. The society grew exponentially in just ten years to a membership of seven hundred in 1851. Among the prominent members then were Daniel McAvoy, Longworth's gardener who laid out the Garden of Eden; Nicholas Longworth; John P. Foote; Dr. J.A. Warder; William Resor; and many other prominent citizens.

The American Winegrowers' Association of Cincinnati came next, founded in 1851 as an outgrowth of the Cincinnati Horticultural Society. It was modeled on the German *Wein Bau Verbesserungs Gesellschaft* (Wine

JOHN P. FOOTE.   A.H.ERNST.   F. PENTLAND.   S.S.JACKSON   DᴿJ.A.WARDER.
                                         E.J.HOOPER.   J.SAYER.

GABRIEL SLEATH. GEO.GRAHAM.R.BUCHANAN   N.LONGWORTH.

Longworth sits with other founding members and winemakers of the Cincinnati Horticultural Society in this portrait. *Courtesy of the Public Library of Cincinnati and Hamilton County.*

Farmers' Improvement Society) to promote the cultivation of the grape, the preparation of wine in its greatest purity and the encouragement of such efforts. The society was to measure the specific gravity of wines and record their properties and qualities. By 1859, Ohio was the top producer of wine in America. We had truly achieved and deserved the "Rhine of America" moniker.

The Winegrowers' Association held monthly meetings, visited vineyards, discussed techniques and, of course, tasted local wines. Members held a wine tasting of forty-five different wines at their first meeting on March 29, 1851, and by 1853, they were using the 100 point rating system still in use today in wine judging.

In 1846, Dr. Melzer Flagg prepared an extensive report to the Cincinnati Horticultural Society documenting the growers, size of vineyards and harvest yields. This began the first extensive records for grape crops during the Catawba Craze. Flagg's Hyde Park farm on Edwards Road, with 3 acres of vineyard, abutted the Rookwood estate of Joseph Longworth, Nicholas's only son. Flagg reported eighty-three vineyards, encompassing 250 acres,

114 acres in bearing, producing twenty-three thousand gallons of wine. Most of the vineyards were small, under 2 acres in size, but Flagg denoted that seventeen were of moderate size—between 3 and 5 acres. There were only nine vineyards larger than 5 acres. Longworth had the largest with 22 acres. His Garden of Eden vineyards had just been planted in 1844 and were not yet in bearing. Flagg mentioned that over half of the crop had been ruined by an early spring frost and subsequent rot. But despite this, he said there was great potential for wine in Cincinnati, with good soil, fair exposure and a favorable climate, comparing it to the best wine regions of France and Spain. He estimated an average yield of Cincinnati vineyards to be five hundred gallons per acre. The only problem, he said, was that most of the vintners were amateurs and needed the proper training in terracing, tilling the soil and caring for the tender young vines.

The 1846 report gives us a perspective on the volumes and growth during the Catawba Craze, with thirty-five thousand gallons of wine made that year. Although the reports are not consistent in their methods or values, nor are they specific in breaking down type of grape or type of wine, we can at least see the dramatic rise in volume and size of the market compared to other areas of the country. In 1849, there were seventy-five thousand gallons of wine pressed in Hamilton County. In 1850, the Cincinnati Horticultural Society initiated another report on winemaking, this time extending the reach to a twenty-mile radius around Cincinnati, not just Hamilton County. It reported 264 proprietors (from the 83 only five years prior) and 750 acres of vineyards. The average cost of planting a one-acre vineyard was estimated at $200, and the annual yield was estimated at two hundred gallons per acre, which Bogen and large winemakers like Longworth easily surpassed.

In 1851, there were 1,000 acres in vines, and the industry was employing about five hundred people and worth about $150,000. By 1855, there were 1,200 acres of vineyards, with 800 in bearing, and a production of 320,000 gallons. The height of the Catawba Craze came four years later in 1859, when there were 2,000 acres of vineyards producing 568,000 gallons of wine. The good growing years in the 1850s and the guerrilla marketing of Longworth had motivated many small and amateur growers to get into the Catawba game.

The Ohio Agricultural Censuses of 1850 and 1860 give us more good data points, especially for the Delhi township area, which was the epicenter of grape growing during the Catawba Craze. At that time (1862), there were three thousand acres of vineyards in Cincinnati, about seven-eighths of which was in Catawba.

What also drove the Catawba Craze was that there was more demand for Catawba still and sparkling wine than there were grapes to supply it. By 1857, the Longworth Wine House had bought the majority of its grapes from Missouri growers. And in 1858, it sourced twenty-five thousand gallons of juice from grapes grown in Brown County, Ohio, because of the lack of supply from Hamilton County growers. That year, Brown County surpassed Hamilton County's wine production by three thousand gallons, marking the decline in growership and production in Cincinnati.

The nurseries that supplied vine cuttings and seedlings to growers were like the dry goods stores during the California Gold Rush that supplied the pickaxes and pans to the miners. They didn't mine the gold or grow the grapes, but they made a lot of money on those who did. One of the largest and the oldest in Cincinnati was the business of James McCullough and Sons. James was born in Sycamore Township in 1811 on the farm of his father, Sampson McCullough, who had come to Cincinnati from Pennsylvania as a surveyor in 1795. He established his seed business in 1838, later incorporating his son, Albert, with a warehouse at 136 Walnut Street and nurseries in Norwood. They provided seeds for lawn, field and garden and grapevine cuttings all over the United States; they even exported to Europe. Their seed catalogue was one of the most prominent in America. The original home and nursery is now Lindner Park & McCullough Estate Nature Preserve in the city of Norwood. Daniel McAvoy's Garden of Eden seed business was another prominent fixture.

By the end of the Civil War, large grape growing had moved toward the Lake Erie region. By 1867, there were 7,000 acres of vineyards in Sandusky and the Lake Erie Islands. In 1873 in Ohio, 208,000 gallons of wine were pressed from 19,660 acres of vineyards. By 1889, there were 33,000 acres of vineyards in Ohio, with the majority being in the Lake Erie counties.

While there was a variety of business models for grape growers, Cincinnati produced multiple brands of native wine. Small grape growers sold to big wine houses like Werk's or Longworth's that had their own presses. Others made their own non-branded wines for community sale or even as currency to pay workers. Some sold their grapes at market to makers of homemade wine for personal consumption. Cincinnati native wine brands included Queen Victoria Brand of Charles Schumann of Riverside. Michael Werk produced the Golden Eagle, Red Cross and Sunset brands of still and sparkling red and white wines from his Westwood and Lake Erie wineries. Fournier, Longworth's sparkling wine manager, produced his own Cabinet and Golden Medal Sparkling Catawba Wines. Nicholas Longworth's premium

Sparkling Catawba brand was called Golden Wedding. John Mottier of Delhi Township produced National Premium Catawba Wine. Egbert Thompson produced Hillside branded wines from Latonia, Kentucky. The Benedictine brothers of Monte Cassino produced Red Rose brand. Jean Corneau of Latonia produced the Cornucopia brand. Christian Schneicke, Longworth's best grower in the Garden of Eden, made an Abe Lincoln brand wine.

Cincinnati's precarious river valley weather wreaked havoc on the grape harvests. The earliest recordings of severe late spring frosts affecting grapes were that of April 26, 1834, and May 9, 1838. Dr. John Warder reported in 1845 that of the eighty-three vineyards in 350 acres in Hamilton County, twenty-one were substantially injured by the late frost of May 7. The good dry years were 1846, 1848 and 1851, with an average of 300 gallons to the acre. A late frost on April 15, 1849, lowered the average yield per acres to 100 gallons of 360 acres of vineyards. The year 1850 scarcely saw any rot, with an average yield of 400 gallons to the acre. A severe frost of January and February 1852 killed many of the grape buds in warm exposed situations and nearly decimated all vineyards in Kentucky. The year 1853 was the most favorable for the grape crop since 1848, and the yield was unusually large—the average was about 650 gallons per acre from the best cultivated vineyards, as well as 800 to 900 gallons from a few. Then 1864 brought a particularly bad year for rot.

The Cincinnati Horticultural Society had been tasting and judging local members' wines from its founding. In 1846, it began giving a coveted silver cup for first premium wine awards at its annual fall exhibition. The first best wine was given in 1843 to John Mottier's 1837 Vintage Catawba. Also noted as a good wine that year was the 1839 Catawba wine of Jacob Resor. The first premium of 1846 for vintage 1845 was given to Gabriel Sleath and the second premium to Louis Rehfuss. Christian Schneicke's 1847 Catawba wine won the silver cup in 1848 out of thirty-six bottles. It was the first wine he made in America from his first grape crop in his Garden of Eden vineyards and was made from his own designed and built press. Some might say beginner's luck, but he continued to win awards and acclaim for his wines. Thomas Yeatman won the silver cup in 1849 for the vintage of 1848 out of fifty-one bottles. First premium of 1850 went to Yeatman and 1851 to Mottier. At the New York State Fair in Rochester in September 1851, Gabriel Sleath won the best 1850 vintage (Rehfuss, second), Robert Buchanan the best 1849 (Corneau, second) and Sebastian Rentz the best 1848 vintage. First premiums went to Michael Werk in 1854 and 1855. In 1856, the society gave the silver goblet to Sebastian Rentz for best Catawba wine. The last awards the society gave were a silver service worth $350 in 1868 to Lewis Finch for Best Wine Grape in America for his Ives crop and a silver goblet worth $100 to E.A. Thompson for Best Wine Grape of Ohio for his Concord.

In 1846, an analysis by a Dr. Chapman of the Catawba wines made by Longworth and Rentz showed them to have an alcohol content of more than 11 percent, while the Hock wines of Germany they were compared to contained only 7.5 percent alcohol. So even though Longworth promoted wines as a temperance beverage, they packed a larger alcoholic punch than their Germanic counterparts.

THE BOGEN BROTHERS:
LONGWORTH'S BIGGEST COMPETITORS

Longworth's biggest competitors were Germanic immigrants George (1810–1882) and Peter Bogen (1812–1888). The brothers were born to miller Jakob Bogen and Louisa Lang in Kleinkarlbach, Bad Dürkheim, in the Rheinland-Pfalz region of Germany. The family came in 1826, first settling in Germantown, Ohio. Two years later, Jakob rented a small farm from Nicholas Longworth where they raised vegetables for market. Their first landlord would become their friendly competitor in another fifteen years.

In 1830, the two brothers took livestock farming to another level, creating a meatpacking business on Hamilton Road near the Brighton House. Their hams, cured meats and sausages became very popular among the German American immigrant community in Cincinnati; they butchered as many as 180 hogs per day.

Peter married Willhemina Schatzmann in 1835, and George married Maria Magdalena Hatmaker in about 1832. Both had large families.

After their meatpacking business was well established, the brothers sought land for another business venture: winemaking. At a sheriff's auction in 1844, they bought the 105-acre defaulted farm of James DeFelhorn in Hartwell for $3,160. They added a 20-acre lot from their neighbors John and James Slevin for $1,200 and then bought more acreage to total 159 acres, planting 5 acres of vineyards. They named their new estate Hartwell Heights.

To the existing two-and-a-half-story main house they built two one-story stone wings divided into apartments for the extended family who lived on the farm; 25 feet below the house, they built a wine cellar with walls 7 feet

Brothers George (*left*) and Peter Bogen produced still and sparkling wines in commercial quantities during the Catawba Craze. *Courtesy of the Public Library of Cincinnati and Hamilton County.*

thick and 142 feet long to temper the climate for winemaking. Once the grapes were harvested, they were brought into the north wing of the house for pressing. Then the juice was filtered down in a series of pipes to the north end of the wine cellar. The juice was loaded into wooden barrels that were then taken to the south side of the cellar for fermentation and storage. The cellar had fifteen four-hundred-gallon casks and eight one-thousand-gallon casks. Additionally, there were more than one thousand bottles of wine in storage. Once the wine was ready for consumption, it was sent to the meatpacking plant in Brighton and sold for as much as $1.50 per gallon. The leftover must and filtrate not used for wine was used to make Catawba brandy.

The brothers quickly established themselves as a local winemaking force, expanding their operations over the next five years from the start in 1845. They produced 1,110 gallons in 1848, 2,100 in 1849 and 3,300 in 1850. By 1850, they had expanded their plantings to fifteen acres of vineyard, with ten in bearing. They produced 500 gallons of wine per acre, nearly double the average productivity of Cincinnati-area vineyards. In 1854, they expanded vineyards to another tract in Carthage and one in Green Township, totaling

The Bogen homestead is now the Evergreen Retirement Community in Carthage, Ohio. *Courtesy of the author.*

thirty-five acres. They even had an experimental vineyard in the fertile bottoms of the Millcreek not far from their Brighton slaughterhouse. They used slaughter refuse and boiled ground bones as fertilizer on these vineyards. The main Hartwell fifteen-acre vineyard contained four rows of four-foot-thick stone-walled terraces, each seven feet high with steps in between.

Not only did the Bogens grow native Catawba grapes, but they also grew Ives, Norton, Delaware and Alexander (or Cape) grapes, the grapes from Vevay that Longworth had first grown. The Bogens showed their Cape, Sparkling Catawba, Dry Catawba and Old Catawba wines at the 1859 Cincinnati Horticultural Fair, along with other local winemakers Henry Brachman, Michael Werk, John Mottier, Christian Schniecke and James Eshelby. Bogen said that the Norton never yielded half as much as the Catawba in its favorable seasons. The Bogens shared their accounting for the Norton grape. In 1863, from one and a half acres, they made five hundred gallons of wine, selling at $3 per gallon; sold 1,200 cuttings and roots for $2,700; and had expenses of $100. This netted $2,600 for the year, or $1,733 per acre of vineyard. In 1864, the same vineyard netted

$2,300 in earnings, or $1,500 per acre. They also grew the Delaware on one-third of an acre, from which they sold eighty-seven gallons of wine at $6 per gallon, sold cuttings and roots for $2,500 and had an expense of only $22 to care for the vineyard. This netted $3,000 in revenue, or $1,000 per acre. In 1871, George Bogen said that the Rogers Hybrid #15 was the best American grape, even after he had tried the Ives, which was by then considered the local favorite.

The Blight of 1863 affected the Bogens' vineyard, but they soldiered on, while others stopped growing grapes. George decided to divest from the vineyard, and Peter became the sole owner of Hartwell Heights. Peter Bogen also sent his still and Sparkling Catawba and red wines for exhibition at the 1873 International Expo in Vienna, Austria, along with other Cincinnati winemakers Michael Werk, E. Thompson and John Mottier. Dr. John Warder, president of the Horticultural Society, was the state commissioner for the exhibition.

By 1875, Peter was only producing a trickle of wine, and he sold the business to his sons-in-law, Jacob and John Pfau, for $146,000. The Pfau brothers continued to grow all the grape varietals with which Peter Bogen had been successful, and they also supplied local whiskeys through their retail business at 258 Main Street, which they had established in 1855. Both Pfau brothers had died by 1883; their father-in-law outlived them by five years. The Pfau family would own the Hartwell Heights estate for another sixty years. After operating it as a dairy, they leased it to a real estate developer, who then developed it into the Evergreen Retirement Community and Williamstown Apartments in the 1960s.

Franz Hellfereich and the Sweetwine Community

Franz Hellfereich (1816–1865) was an immigrant from Speyer in the Rheinland-Pfalz, who came to Cincinnati in 1841 and formed a winemaking community called Sweetwine on the East Side of Cincinnati. It spanned from Kellogg Avenue up along Five Mile Road Creek Valley to the top of Five Mile Hill, about twelve miles from Cincinnati. He originally called the area Wineburg, and he grew grapes, made his own wine and operated a sort of wine house and resort that was very popular with Cincinnatians. Soon other German immigrants flocked to the area to grow grapes on the southeastern-facing hillsides, and it became a community of Germanic winegrowers. Franz became the first postmaster and mayor of Sweetwine.

Franz decided that there was more money to be made in selling the wines rather than making them. So, in 1859, he sold his wine business in Sweetwine and headed back downtown, where he opened a wholesale wine and liquor business called the Senate Exchange, right across from the courthouse.

Longworth documented a visit to Sweetwine in 1849:

> *This day I visited a German settlement on the Ohio, commencing about twelve miles above the city and extending about four miles. The hill commences close to the river, and rises gradually; the usual bottom-land being on the opposite side of the river. The soil is porous and well calculated, in my opinion, for the cultivation of the grape, and nearly the whole of the four miles is occupied by vineyards, and there are also some on the top of the hill. Two of the vineyards belong to Englishmen; the owners of all the others are Germans.*

CHARLES REEMELIN: FRIEND OF THE WINE COUNTRY KING

Charles Gustav Reemelin (1814–1891) was born into a family of some wealth in Heilbronn in Baden-Wuertemburg, son of Gottlieb and Caroline Reemelin, and came to Cincinnati in 1833, at the very beginning of our Catawba Craze. He saw the earliest vineyards—those of Germanic immigrant brothers Gottlieb and Johann Myers in what is now Hyde Park, Longworth's Bald Hill Vineyards in Tusculum and those of Swiss immigrant (via Vevay, Indiana) Fredrick Diserens, owner of the William Tell Exchange bar downtown. Reemelin was considered one of the German Nobilaten, along with Louis Rehfuss. He spent part of his life as a dry goods merchant downtown but bought a farm in the country in Dent and commuted back and forth. He served as editor of the *Volksblatt*, a Democratic-leaning German newspaper in Cincinnati, and was heavily involved in local politics.

As a young single man in Cincinnati, Reemelin hung out at the Wine House and Tavern, operated by his friends Johann Jakob and Barbara Schweitzerhof. Johann had been drill sergeant in 1827 for a regiment of seven hundred boys in military exercises ordered by the king of Wuertemburg. In 1836, Johann was drill sergeant for the Lafayette Guards, of which Reemelin was a member. Barbara had been a servant for ten years in a family in Heilbronn related to Reemelin. They immigrated to Cincinnati around the same time he did in 1833. Reemelin reminisced, "When I arrived [in

Cincinnati], they were keeping a good boarding house; and her good cooking, and his strict order, made it a very pleasant resort for very many of us young gents. We got there many a good meal; such as our mothers used to provide. I spent many a pleasant hour with them." They were neighbors of the Reemelins for thirty-five years in Dent and cultivated a vineyard, from which Barbara made eight hundred gallons of wine in 1860.

Carl Gustav Rümelin.

A portrait of winemaker and politician Carl Gustav Reemelin. *Courtesy of Green Township Historical Society.*

When Reemelin lived downtown in the 1830s, he was a Fifth Street neighbor of winemaker Herman Duhme. He was also a friend of Westwood winemaker Michael Werk. During an 1843 trip to visit relatives in Germany, he met Werk's father in Strasbourg, giving him a daguerreotype of his son.

Growing up working in his father's vineyards in Heilbronn, Reemelin developed a passion for winemaking that he carried with him to Cincinnati, planting a 9-acre vineyard of Catawba grapes on his 105-acre Dent farm under the guidance of his neighbor Frank Frohndorf. Reemelin built his house on the farm in 1851. He had whittled down his holdings by sale to 32 acres by 1890. In 1859, Reemelin sold the farm in Dent and moved downtown to Vine between Ninth and Court, but he bought back the farm in 1862, after which he worked to reinvigorate the vineyards that the former owner had let fall into disrepair. By 1875, he was making less revenue from his vineyard and doing the work himself, which he was feeling he was too old for. As a local farmer, he participated in the Harvest Home Festival in Cheviot for twenty years, speaking at the festival about his *History of Green Township* work in 1881.

His writings on grape culture for the *Ohio Farmer* caught the eye of a New York publisher, who gave him $700 to organize them in book form, which became *The Vine Dressers Manual.* He preferred book writing over what he called his "gratuitous contributions to newspapers." Then, in 1869, he wrote *The Winemakers Manual.* Both books got wide acclaim as manuals for even the inexperienced grower. In them he recommended the best soil (trenched limestone mixed with gravel versus clay), south-facing slopes instead of pastures, locations near anything like a forest to temper raw wind and frost and the importance of specific pruning and weeding of the vineyard.

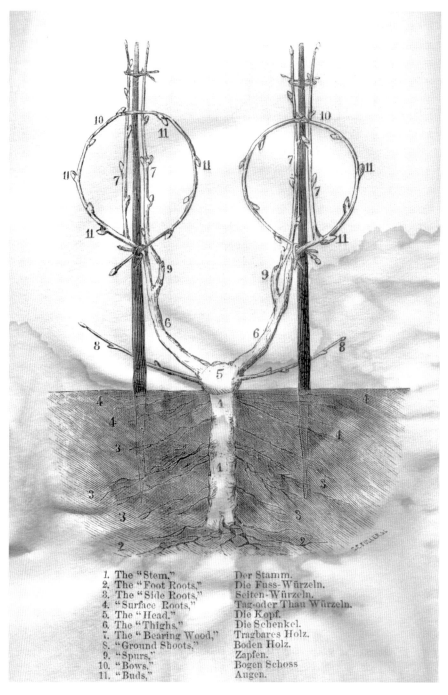

1. The "Stem,"	Der Stamm.
2. The "Foot Roots,"	Die Fuss-Würzeln.
3. The "Side Roots,"	Seiten-Würzeln.
4. "Surface Roots,"	Tag-oder Thau Würzeln.
5. The "Head."	Die Kopf.
6. The "Thighs,"	Die Schenkel.
7. The "Bearing Wood,"	Tragbares Holz.
8. "Ground Shoots,"	Boden Holz.
9. "Spurs,"	Zapfen.
10. "Bows,"	Bogen Schoss
11. "Buds,"	Augen.

A diagram of a proper, staked, pruned and bowed grapevine from Charles Reemelin's 1856 *Vine Dresser's Guide. Courtesy of the German Heritage Museum.*

Although our modern trellising was becoming the standard in the Palatinate and Rhineland in Germany, Reemelin was emphatic that the round bending and staking was the best way to train vines. He said that bending the bearing wood promotes its bearing qualities, preventing rapid upflow of sap, which creates too prolific a growth that wearies the wood and prevents good grape bearing. He recommended the wine press made by local fabricator Miles Greenwood.

While growing the Catawba grape, Reemelin thrice imported grapes from Baden. He mentioned that the Riesling was the popular grape in Germany when he left in the 1830s, but by 1850, it was the Traminer. He tried to grow imported German gooseberries, with no success, but he was successful in growing pears, apricots, plums and raspberries. He recommended growing the Catawba, and possibly the Isabella, and also recommended an area for a grapevine nursery to sell cuttings, which was very profitable.

Reemelin's family had personal ties to Wilhelm I, the king of Baden-Wuertemburg. Knowing this connection, Longworth in 1854 asked him for a huge favor on one of his frequent trips to visit relatives in Germany. He wanted a testimonial from the king, the royal of the world's best winemaking region. He could promote this royal endorsement to increase his brand recognition. Queen Victoria had just visited the wineries around Hockenheim, Germany, in 1851 and put her royal stamp on them as the best. The name Hock wine was taken from this and applied to still Catawba wines to market them in the same class as these superior German wines. The Germans from wine country would have used their traditional green Hock wine glasses, now called Roemer glasses, to drink this wine.

Reemelin's grandmother had been a frequent visitor to the court of Wilhelm's second wife, Queen Catherine, in Ludwigsburg, and his brother-in-law, married to Reemelin's eldest sister, Lina, was marshal of the king's palace. Reemelin used this connection and had the wine delivered to the king on his birthday. The king, Queen Pauline and their court enjoyed the wine. Upon returning from this trip, Reemelin sold his Dent wine crop for $580.

Reemelin wrote in 1871 a frank history of vineyards in Cincinnati. In it he reveals a most accurate account of the rise and fall of our local wine industry from the perspective of the German vine dressers. He noted that the secondary cause of our disasters was large, poorly cultivated vineyards. Vines were dug in holes like trees, instead of being trenched. All the vine dressers knew that there were better, but more laborious, methods. But they were renters and took the advice of Longworth not to trench. They focused more on potatoes and cabbage crops, for which they received full profit, instead of the split of the grape harvest with Longworth. Most of the vineyards in Cincinnati were planted before 1850, and by the time better methods were known from local experience and from Europe, it was hard to correct the mistakes of the past. Along with phylloxera and bad weather seasons, as well as a change in wine and alcohol tastes after the Civil War, this led to the demise of our industry, according to Reemelin. He praised his friend Rehfuss for bringing science into both the growing and winemaking processes for the improvement of our local wines.

Reemelin lamented that the homestead and vineyards he thought he was creating as a legacy to pass on to his children would be lost. None of his children wanted to be farmers and vineyardists, and he sold off his land in Dent and built a house in Cincinnati. He passed out his Catawba wine to buyers at the auction of his estate in 1890 and toasted the sale with it before they left Dent for good. He took his last three barrels of vintage 1889 Catawba wine with him to his new downtown home.

LOUIS REHFUSS: CHRISTMAS TREES AND SACCHAROMETERS

Dr. Ludwig (Louis) Rehfuss (1806–1855) was another of the "Dreissiger Nobilaten," like Reemelin. These were liberal intellectuals who emigrated from the Germanic kingdoms in the 1830s to escape political persecution. Many of these political Dreissiger happened to be winemakers.

Rehfuss was born in Ebingen, Baden-Wuertemburg, the son of wealthy merchant Johann Rehfuss. After graduating with a degree in medicine from the University of Tuebingen, he came to Cincinnati in 1833 and set up the wholesale pharmacy business of Rehfuss and Kolb at the corner of Fifth and Vine Streets, at today's Fountain Square. With his political activist nature, he helped to create the Cincinnati *Volksblatt* newspaper in 1836, the voice of the Democratic-leaning Dreissiger and the poor and articulate Germanic farmers. Their local hangout was the Wine Bar of Johann Jakob Schweitzerhof. Rehfuss is also credited as the one who brought the Christmas tree to Cincinnati in the 1830s and for the formation of the Cincinnati Symphony Orchestra.

As a president of the Winegrowers' Association, Rehfuss hosted meetings and wine tastings at his house in the 1850s. His contribution to local winemaking was the use of the saccharometer to measure sugar content of grapes and the final alcoholic strength. Longworth highly advocated for its use. Rehfuss also advocated for the practice of mineral manuring of grapevines, which he said improved their flavor and reduced tannins. He had a very public feud with Longworth's sparkling wine manager Fournier in the horticultural journals over this. Rehfuss staged blind tastings of manured versus non-manured grape wines with the Winegrowers' Association, proving his theories.

DR. JOHN ASTON WARDER: EARLY ENVIRONMENTALIST AND MASTER VINEYARDIST

Dr. John Aston Warder was one of the several doctors turned vineyardists in Cincinnati during the height of the Catawba Craze. Although he is more known for his contributions to American forestry, he had a huge impact on the local and national wine industry with his numerous writings. He was truly a Renaissance man like many of the other Cincinnati capitalist winemakers.

Dr. Warder was born in Philadelphia, Pennsylvania, in 1812, the eldest son of wealthy intellectual Quakers Jeremiah and Ann Aston Warder. His parents were also avid horticulturists and frequently hosted prominent men of the field like John James Audubon at their suburban estate, Woodside. In 1830, when Warder was an eighteen-year-old considering college, his family relocated west to Springfield, Ohio, where Jeremiah had inherited land from his father. He graduated in 1836 from Jefferson Medical College in Philadelphia. In 1837, he married Elizabeth Browne Haines from Germantown, Pennsylvania, and moved to Cincinnati to practice medicine. His practice was located at the Newport Ferry on the corner of Ludlow and Front Streets.

DR. JOHN A. WARDER.

An illustration of Dr. John Aston Warder. *Courtesy of the Public Library of Cincinnati and Hamilton County.*

In 1844, Warder purchased a twenty-nine-acre estate in Clifton, off Lafayette Avenue, which he named Scarlet Oaks, after his favorite oak tree. He planted a vineyard and scarlet oak trees on his and neighbors' property. For this his neighbors nicknamed him the "Medical Johnny Appleseed." Warder grew Catawba, Hartford Prolific and Ives grapes. He built a beautiful cottage there and raised a family of seven children for a decade.

In 1855, Warder decided to give up his medical practice and join his local capitalist buddies to

An 1850s lithograph of Dr. Warder's Gothic home in Clifton, which he named Scarlet Oaks. *Courtesy of the Public Library of Cincinnati and Hamilton County.*

devote all his time to horticulture. He purchased more than three hundred acres near North Bend, Ohio, between River and Bridgetown Roads from President William Henry Harrison's widow, Anne. He moved his family from their Clifton residence into a frame house on his property with an amazing Rhine River–like view of the western bend in the Ohio River. He then started building his English manor house he would call Aston, after his mother's family. Beyond fruit orchards of a huge variety of apples and pears, he made plantings of ornamental trees and shrubs, of which he made a systematic study during the following years. Essentially, Aston became the first agricultural experimental station in the United States.

Warder became involved with the Cincinnati Horticultural Society, the Cincinnati Society of Natural History, the Ohio Horticultural Society, the Ohio State Board of Agriculture and the Western Academy of Natural Sciences and served on the boards of the Winegrowers' Association, local schools and various other organizations. Warder helped draw public attention to gardening and landscape design, advocating for the beautification of parks and cemeteries. He was one of the founders and designers of Spring Grove Cemetery.

Unlike the other Cincinnati vineyardists who wrote books on the subject, Warder was no one-hit wonder. He wrote books, articles and pamphlets about winemaking for more than two decades. From 1850 to 1853, he edited the *Western Horticultural Review*, devoted to horticulture, grape culture and winemaking. Through this journal, Warder advanced knowledge in proper setup, care, choice of grape variety and winemaking techniques. In 1867, Dr. Warder edited a book written in French by Dr. Alphonse du Breuil, a leading authority on French vineyards. In it Warder presented the first extensive analysis of the profitability of the wine industry in Europe compared to America. He compiled the first list of 170 known American grapes. And he described the known vine pests in a Dr. Seussian lineup, from Spotted Winged Sable to the Eight Spotted Forrester.

Warder declared that if we couldn't make pure wines without adding sugar, we should not be in the wine industry. This was an early debate among the early Cincinnati winemakers. Some believed that adding sugar to make sweeter wines diminished the foxiness of the grape, a taste that turned many off to American wines. Longworth was on the "no sugar added" side of that debate.

Dr. John Aston Warder's house, Aston, in North Bend, Ohio, as it is today. *Courtesy of the author.*

Warder was honored with a grape varietal named for him, the Dr. Warder. It was a red *Vitus labrusca*, of unknown parentage, from Theophile Huber of Illinois City, Illinois. Warder's North Bend residence still stands, with its commanding view of the Ohio River, and his farm is now the Aston Oaks subdivision.

ROBERT BUCHANAN: DRY GOODS, PIGS AND CATAWBA WINE

Robert Buchanan (1797–1879), of Scottish descent, was one of the rich capitalists who had a winemaking side hustle. He was a cousin of President James Buchanan and was born outside Pittsburgh in the backwoods of Pennsylvania. His early career was in the dry goods and pork packing markets, coming to Cincinnati in 1820. He started the Phoenix Cotton Mills and later the Covington Cotton Mills. He then became partner in a firm for steam engine mills for sugar plantations, became involved in the Little Miami Railroad and the Whitewater Canal and was president of the Cincinnati Commercial Bank for five years. He was president of the Cincinnati Horticultural Society and the American Winegrowers' Association, hosting many meetings at his Clifton estate.

In 1843, Buchanan chose a commanding forty-five-acre site in Clifton off Ludlow Avenue for his Green Hill estate. He planted fruit orchards and planted a six-acre vineyard of 14,400 vines (of Catawba, Cape, Isabella and Lenoir grapes) using the spur and bow method. He received best Catawba wine vintage 1849 at the 1851 New York State Fair in Rochester, and his wine earned a spot on the menu at Cincinnati's high-end Gibson Hotel in 1856, alongside Marcobrunner and Rudesheimer German Hock Wines.

Robert Buchanan was president of the Cincinnati Horticultural Society, a grower and a winemaker, and he wrote a book on grape culture. *Courtesy of the Public Library of Cincinnati and Hamilton County.*

In 1853, Buchanan wrote a book titled *The Culture of the Grape*, in three editions. In it, he documented the native grape varietals that winemakers were growing in Cincinnati: the Catawba, Isabella, Cape, Bland's Madeira, Ohio/Cigar Box, Lenoir, Missouri, Norton, Herbemont, Minor's Seedling, White Catawba and Mammouth Catawba. He assembled the writings of Nicholas Longworth, Reyfuss, Resor and several others into one guidebook with annotations for the serious grower of native grapes.

In 1865, he was one of the several who defended Cincinnati as a wine growing region from Yeatman's scathing treatise against it and urged growers to convert hardier grapes than the Catawba. His Green Hill house still stands in Clifton.

Jacob Resor: From Gunmaking to Fermentation

Among Buchanan's Clifton neighbors were sons of Jacob Resor (1784–1845), another wealthy capitalist who became proficient at winemaking. The Reuben and William Resor (1810–1874) houses are at 3517 Cornell Place and 254 Greendale Avenue. Jacob Resor's first-year 1837 Catawba was said to be "of good capacity and with age will become of high character by the Cincinnati Horticultural Society," and his Cape wines were highly spoken of in 1843.

Jacob Resor came from a long line of gunsmiths and locksmiths from Elsoff, Wittgenstein, in today's German state of Westphalia. His grandfather Matthias escaped Wittgenstein in the late 1830s to America with his friend Peter Heger (founder of Hagerstown, Maryland), without the permission of the Duke Ludwig I of Hesse-Darmstadt and Westphalia, for whom they worked as gunsmiths. Jacob came to Cincinnati by flatboat in 1811, establishing a thriving tin and copper smithing business. By 1819, Jacob and his two sons, William and Reuben, were manufacturing stoves. They received a patent for the Resor cooking stove in 1835, opening Cincinnati's first stove factory. Prior to the Civil War, their stoves were known nationally for their style, fuel efficiency and durability.

Jacob's daughter, Julia, befriended another winemaker's daughter at the Young Ladies' Seminary in Cincinnati. She became lifelong friends with Julia Dinsmore, whose father, James Dinsmore, grew Catawba grapes and made wine in his estate near Burlington, Kentucky. James sold grape cuttings from his vineyard and in 1860 produced three hundred gallons of wine, using it mostly to pay his farm laborers.

William Resor reported on his father's vineyards to the Cincinnati Horticultural Society. He planted in 1834 1,774 vines of Cape, Catawba and Isabella, which cost him $284 to plant and $50 in labor per year. He averaged 480 gallons per acre from 1837 to 1845. With more vines planted during that year, the final count of vines in 1845 was 2,300. Resor was one of the earliest Catawba grape growers, after Longworth, in Cincinnati.

HERMAN DUHME: MUCH ADO ABOUT FLATWARE

Herman Heinrich Duhme (1819–1888) was born in Ueffeln Osnabruck, Germany, in 1819 and came to Ohio in 1834. He and his brother John (1816–1853) started a fancy goods and variety store in 1843 on Main and Walnut Streets. Duhme & Company began producing its own jewelry and silver wares around 1866. Although not a silversmith himself, Herman employed a number of silversmiths and jewelers and produced a wide range of silver table wares and jewelry, eventually becoming the most prolific and prominent silver manufacturer in the Midwest. Duhme & Company survived Herman's death in 1888 in Michigan, changing ownership and names several times until it finally closed in 1910.

H.H. Duhme amassed a fortune in stoves and silver industries to fund his vineyards and winemaking at his estate in Riverside, east of downtown Cincinnati. *Courtesy of the Public Library of Cincinnati and Hamilton County.*

Herman was like other wealthy business barons and upper-class white-collar workers who had acreage in the country outside Cincinnati and commuted to their factory or offices downtown. His gentleman's farm was in Riverside, below what is now Mount St. Joseph College, and he commuted daily to his downtown jewelry store at Fourth and Walnut Streets. His estate was also one of the largest of the Catawba barons, with twelve acres of Catawba vines. In the 1840s, he had a great wine cellar built underneath his large home, and by the 1850s, he was pressing ten thousand gallons of wine a season.

Herman Duhme's wines were some of the earliest from Cincinnati to win national recognition. Along with other Cincinnati wine barons like Buchanan, Corneau, Schumann and Yeatman, he showed Catawba wines at the 1851 World's Fair held in London from May 1 to October 15 at the beautiful Crystal Palace, built by Prince Albert. Duhme and Charles Schuman, both of Riverside, won European recognition for their Musk Catawba still wines. The royal commissioners awarded them each a medal of merit for these wines. Duhme became a member of the American Winegrowers' Association in 1852.

SEBASTIAN FEY AND HIS LEGACY

Meier Winery had another competitor in the Fey Winery, located at 2287–2289 Colerain Avenue and Zinck Alley. It was the successor to the Fey wine enterprise in Cincinnati, founded in 1847 and operated until 1963. At that time, it was Cincinnati's oldest continually operating winery and vineyard, with a capacity of sixty thousand gallons.

There were two main wine businesses passed down from Sebastian Fey (1812–1870) to his four sons. The first was the wine house and cellars at Vine and Green Streets, which operated from 1850 until Prohibition in 1920. Then there was the vineyard and wine house at Colerain Avenue in Brighton, which operated from about 1870 to 1963. Both businesses claimed as their birthdate Sebastian's date of arrival in Cincinnati in 1846, rather than the founding of his first wine house in Carthage in 1847.

Sebastian Fey was born in the Rheinland-Pfalz region of Germany in Kirchheim an der Eck on December 18, 1812. He was son of Johann Michael Fey, a miller and farmer, and Regina Fey. He was called away for military service to the king for six years and was lucky to find a job in the department of genetics until 1844; there he dealt with both livestock breeding and plant hybridization. This is where his interest in viticulture was born. And with this knowledge and all of the propaganda at the time enticing Germans to immigrate to America, he saw the opportunity for a bigger life there. He returned to the farm and married Margaretha Koch in 1845 in Bad Bergzabern, Germany.

Sebastian and his new wife immigrated to the United States in 1846, and he found work with immigrant winemakers George and Peter Bogen at their farm and vineyards in Carthage, Ohio. Here he put his farm skills and genetics knowledge to work and learned how to grow and tend native Catawba, Delaware and other grapes, as well as how to make wine. Sebastian and his wife had four sons who were involved in the wine business: William, Theodore, Louis and Edward. The youngest son's business lasted the longest.

Sebastian saw the opportunity for himself in the wine business, so he quickly traded in his farmer's apron for a saloonkeeper's and opened a wine house in 1847 on the corner of Vine Street and Hamilton Road. He became known as a jovial proprietor and proved to be a fine wine connoisseur and crafter of good wines himself. He became the first to import Rhine wines to Cincinnati in large quantities. His wine cellars held numerous bottles of the best German wines.

The winery of Sebastian Fey, shown here, continued for three generations into the 1960s as one of the oldest surviving Cincinnati wine operations. *Courtesy of the Public Library of Cincinnati and Hamilton County.*

He stayed at the Carthage location for three years and then decided to look for a more central location for his growing business. He bought the property at the northwest corner of Green and Vine Streets in 1850 and built his new wine house in the center of the Over-the-Rhine neighborhood. It had wine presses on the ground floor and three sub-cellars thirty feet deep, where the wine was stored for fermentation in oak vats, but they also owned the vineyard in Brighton at Colerain Avenue and Zinck Alley.

This new location also became a popular gathering place for those who enjoyed a glass of wine. His sons Wilhelm and Theodore inherited their father's natural joviality and his passion for the craft. Under their management, the number of regular customers increased steadily over the next twenty years.

The winemaking at the Vine Street location happened in October, after the fall grape harvest. The third basement cellar was where the newly pressed wine was stored for fermentation. Typically, the cellar door was left open to vent the carbonic acid gases that were a byproduct of fermentation. Before the days of good HVAC systems and SCUBA gear, winemaking could be a precarious business, and a near-fatal miss happened in the Fey wine cellars in 1891.

The third son, Louis Fey (1852–1934), inherited a love for the wine hospitality business and took over the wine store and restaurant of Fred Engel in the 1870s, a few doors down on 477 Vine Street from his father's wine house. He then opened another café at 432 Walnut Street that was noted as being the hub for politicians of both parties in the 1870s.

When Sebastian died, his Vine and Green Street business passed on to sons William (1846–1925) and Theodore (1851–1933), who lived in Clifton Heights. Upon William's retirement in 1908, the winery passed to his sons William Jr. (1880–1948) and Clarence (1880–1949), who ran it until Prohibition.

The fourth son, Edward Fey Sr. (1861–1907), took on the Colerain Avenue winery. As the youngest son, Edward Sr. was the most successful of his brothers in the business and the most knowledgeable as both a vineyardist and a winemaker. He was called on by the Benedictine brothers of the Monte Cassino vineyards in Covington in the 1880s to consult on the best grapes and methods for growing.

Edward Fey Jr. (1881–1941) operated the Colerain Avenue winery in partnership with his sister, Edith Fey Otte, after their father's death. Edward Fey Jr. lived in Indian Hill, where the Ives grape was first cultivated commercially. He also grew the Ives grape on his Brighton Vineyard. By the time Edward passed in 1941, he had built the Colerain Avenue winery to an impressive sixty-thousand-gallon capacity. Edward's sister, Edith, and his widow sold it in 1943 to Arthur J. Hastell of Delhi, who had operated Henri's Wine House downtown since 1936. He and his wife, Gladys, owned it for twenty years, until it was demolished for the construction of Interstate 75 in 1963.

By the end of World War II, the Fey Winery, now under the ownership of the

A 1960s Edward Fey Wine ad touting its longevity of one hundred years in Cincinnati. *Courtesy of the Public Library of Cincinnati and Hamilton County.*

Hastells in Brighton, was making extra dry Catawba and Delaware wines, semi-sweet Catawba and Ives and sweet ports and sherries. Fey and Meier were the first to make Bordeaux French semi-sweet-style Sauterne wines from a mixture of Ohio grapes—Catawba, Delaware and Concord—instead of the standard French Sauvignon Blanc, Sémillion and Muscadelle. It would later be renamed Haute Sauterne. They also made a sparkling wine called Fey's Silver Spray.

A Catawba Vineyardist in Dunlap

About two miles from today's Vinoklet Winery on old Colerain Avenue, in what was once the town of Dunlap, Ohio, sat the 150-acre farm and vineyard of Giles Richards (1792–1876). Richards had migrated to Cincinnati from Cambridge, Massachusetts, in 1816 with his brother Amos Richards, where they worked as agents for the New York Card Manufacturing Company until 1822. Richards's work introduced him to many prominent citizens of Cincinnati, including Nicholas Longworth.

Their father manufactured cotton and wool cards in Cambridge and was a friend and associate of many prominent Boston citizens. Like other vineyardists during the Cincinnati Catawba Craze, Richards had made his money as an entrepreneur, running the Colerain Flouring Mill, the Colerain Cotton Mill, the Fulling and Carding Mill, the Giles Richards Store Concern, a dye house, a tavern house and a sawmill in Colerain. He retired from active business in 1835 and focused his attention on farming.

With the money made from his many business ventures, Richards bought in 1828 the 150-acre farm on River Road at Colerain Pike. He built a house there in 1832 he called Elland after his wife, Eleanor Hankinson Lloyd, and daughter, Elizabeth Adams Richards. The hills sloping toward the Great Miami River were perfect for a vineyard, and by 1840, Richards was making still wine from his vineyards of Catawba and Isabella grapes.

Richards told his brother Thomas about the grape harvest in 1850:

We worked up 21 barrels of grapes after you left, 14 of the first picking and 7 of the second. The barrels that were filled after you left were marked No 1 and 2 on the head with chalk. There is none of the wine done fermenting, but several barrels so near done that I ventured to stop them up by putting the bung in slightly. The weather is too cold for the fermentation to go on fast, particularly upstairs.

He sold his estate-made wine to customers like S.T. Lippincott in New York City, who supplied to a restaurateur to stock their wine cellar. Another potential client in Brooklyn, L.S. Burnham, wrote how native wines had not quite taken in New York in a letter of 1850: "I Beg you will receive my thanks (in the wine) myself and my family are not great wine drinkers, but we like what we do use to be pure and good, which we are assured yours is. Perhaps as the 'native' becomes more abundant, we shall use more."

At the very first Fall Exhibition of the Cincinnati Horticultural Society, the *Western Farmer and Gardener* noted, "Mr. Giles Richards of Colerain sent in his Catawba wine, pronounced by the most distinguished connoisseur present, 'very good.'"

In the late 1830s, Nicholas Longworth had wisely invested $500 in ten shares of the Colerain, Oxford and Brookville Turnpike, of which Richards was the treasurer and president. With that association, Richards often consulted Longworth for advice on grape growing and winemaking. In a letter dated April 22, 1850, Longworth praised him for using a chicken wire bed to successfully keep the rot off his vines and approved of his winemaking process. Longworth recommended Richards show his 1840 vintage at the Fall Exhibition of the Cincinnati Horticultural Society.

On October 16, 1863, Richards wrote to Longworth's best vineyardist, the German immigrant Christian Schniecke, who received his mail at the Gilbert House and lived on Longworth's Garden of Eden. He was in a contract of sale for Richards's grapes for the Longworth Wine House. Richards asked, "What shall I do with the second picking of grapes on the arbor and the Isabella grapes? They will hardly ripen enough to make a first rate wine, but will do as I am told for champagne or sparkling if you will take them I will call them 7 cents per thousand. Please answer if you will take them. They shall be picked carefully and sent in wagons unbraised so that you can sort them as much as you please. There will be a good many good grapes among them."

Richards sold his wine to family and associates in Boston and New York, but his still Rhine wines were not as popular as the sparkling champagnes of Longworth and Bogen, made in Cincinnati. In a letter dated March 29, 1855, Richards's nephew from Boston, Amos Lawrence, wrote: "The other day we had our governor, who is a neighbor of mine, to dinner and some of the other guest officers of the state. And as they were nearly all tee-totalers, my wife had a very fine assortment of homemade drinks. When I use almost altogether on the same principle that we use our own manufactured goods. She even had some American champagne, which lasted very well (Bogen Cincinnati, was the mark on it) and the company finished a couple of bottles of it. Your wine, being more like the Rhine wines did not go so well, though it is always praised."

Nephew Amos would enlist his uncle in November 1855 to endorse a $100 check to Nicholas Longworth for what would have been a decent quantity of wine and ordered another amount of Longworth's still Catawba wine.

Like many vineyardists, Richards also sold his roots. Selling of rootstocks was a hedge sideline to make money even in times of bad weather leading to bad harvests. He sold 1,500 rootstock to A.D. Coombs in the spring of 1850. Coombs successfully planted 1,427 and saw them grow to fruit, but he asked for a two-dollar refund on the only 1,430 he received, 33 of which he said were old and unfit for replanting.

When Richards vacated and left the farm to his daughter and son-in-law, Alfred West Gilbert, after the Civil War, he expected a $100 check for his wine press, which Gilbert had assumed was considered part of the real estate and not a separate entity.

EAST OF HAMILTON COUNTY

During Cincinnati's Catawba Craze, it was said that the eastern Ohio River hills from what's now Coney Island to Ripley, Ohio, formed one continuous vineyard. At the height of its production in the mid-1870s, Brown County produced more than 25,000 barrels of wine annually. In 1858, it produced more wine than Hamilton County. Its growers were an important source of quality grapes for the Longworth Wine House. Hillside river towns to the east of Cincinnati—California, Brachman, Sweetwine, New Richmond, Ravenna, Higginsport and Ripley—were dotted with vineyards, mostly owned by Germanic wine country immigrants.

Clermont County winemakers in 1847 made 12,960 gallons, worth about $6,480. George Weir made 4,800 gallons of Catawba wine from eight acres of land, or 600 gallons to the acre. Thomas Williamson made 1,300 gallons, and William Carnes made 70 gallons on two and a half acres. Charles Ilheart, an immigrant from Berlin, made 150 gallons on an acre. Michael Mae made 240 gallons on two acres. Benjamin Light made about 1,700 gallons on three acres, and Peter Light 1,400 gallons on three acres. In 1873, the county produced 16,581 gallons of wine, indicating that its production was still increasing, even after Cincinnati's was in decline.

John Williamson of New Richmond, Ohio, experimented in the late 1840s with a winemaking process widely practiced in the area of Freiburg in Germany at that time. He let his grapes ferment on the skins slightly after being mashed and before pressing. He let them stand in large open hogsheads for twenty-four to thirty hours, or until they began to ferment and the grapes began to rise to the surface. After that happened, he pressed their juice. Too much fermentation in this state would give a bitter, astringent taste to the wine, but a slight fermentation would add to the color and the aroma. Mr. Williamson's wine made this way enjoyed a high reputation and commanded a price of $1.25 per gallon.

In 1850, Ripley resident Archibald Liggett reported to the Cincinnati Horticultural Society that there were ninety-three acres of vineyards planted with sixteen proprietors, with half of the vines in bearing. In 1848, also a good year in Cincinnati, they made on average about three hundred gallons to the acre, compared to the average six hundred gallons per acre in Cincinnati. Then, in 1849, a bad year, Brown County made one hundred gallons of wine to the acre, equivalent to Cincinnati that year.

Fournier, the manager of Longworth's Sparkling Catawba operations, was responsible for choosing the grapes that the wine house bought. He said in 1858 that Brown County was the best wine growing region in Ohio. The numbers for Brown County vineyards in 1858 were as follows: 17,000 gallons of wine, 3,000 more than Hamilton County. Clermont County vineyards produced 2,500 gallons. The price per gallon ranged from $1 to $1.25—the entire crop was valued at $40,000.

In Higginsport, Ohio, there were growers like Christopher Schnider, listed in 1876 as an estate winemaker. John Groppenbacher also owned a vineyard and made wine in 1876 at his residence outside Higginsport. John was son of German immigrants Mack (1822–1870) and Anna Dart Groppenbacher (1824–1897), who came to Brown County in 1858.

Gottlieb Bambach (1812–1890) was born in Gross Gerau, Germany, near the city of Darmstadt. He was involved in the revolution of 1849 and fled the country in August 1849. He settled at Levanna, Ohio, where he cultivated a vineyard on a 130-acre farm, making 1,500 gallons from his 8-acre vineyard.

Another successful winemaker in Levanna was Johann Georg Kautz (1800–1888), born in Ispringen in Baden-Wuertemburg. He immigrated with his wife, Dorothea Lowing, and young son August in 1828, settling in 1844 on a thirty-six-acre farm in Levanna, where they grew grapes on the hillside and tobacco on the bottoms. He was the second man to engage in winemaking in Brown County, keeping a large wine cellar full of his many vintages of wine. His six sons—August, Fredrick, John, George, Louis and Albert—all served in the Civil War and were known as the "Fighting Kautzes."

AFTER LONGWORTH

O n February 10, 1863, Nicholas Longworth breathed his last breath at the ripe old age of eighty at his house on Pike Street, surrounded by his family. He is said to have called for his son-in-law, William J. Flagg, to tell him that he had finally found a grape that did better than the Catawba. What that grape was we will never know. Longworth never awarded the $500 prize he had advertised for a grape hardier than the Catawba, even though there were certainly hardier grapes. Dr. John Aston Warder, Longworth's Horticultural Society friend, claimed that Longworth often used to say that he should like to have a new lease of life so that he might test more of them, and he felt confident that he should eventually succeed in reaching the desired excellence.

The Cincinnati wine industry lost its biggest cheerleader. The Civil War raged on—many vineyard workers volunteered and were called to fight for the Union, and many didn't come back to work again in the vineyards. Jules and Joseph Masson and Christian Schniecke stayed to operate the wine house for the estate. The Longworth Wine House would not close, at least for several years. There were still wines being aged and an inventory of bottled still and sparkling wines to go through. Even the tenants of Longworth's vineyards had at least the years left on their multi-year tenant contracts to run out—it typically took at least three years for new vines to fruit. Even after his death, some of the vineyard contracts were renewed to guarantee a good supply of grapes to the press house for wine.

One such tenant contract was renewed on April 1, 1864, between Bernard Wintziger and the executors of the Longworth estate:

> *Said Horne and Executors of the Longworth estate agree that said Wintziger shall have the use of two rooms in the Wine House and two acres of ground for a garden until the first day of November next, also half of the cherries from the trees below the Wine House this year and the first two hundred gallons of wine from the vineyard and half the yield for third year if it shall exceed four hundred gallons; and said Wintzger agrees to trim the vines and tie them up and to hoe the ground between them twice thoroughly during the season and also to put any stakes to the vines in the new vineyard that shall be needed the stakes to be provided by said Horne and said Executors of the Longworth Estate.*

Longworth's Garden of Eden would be sold and developed as Eden Park, later housing the Cincinnati Art Museum, the Krohn Conservatory, a drinking water reservoir for the city and Playhouse in the Park.

The Columbia-Tusculum Bald Hill vineyards were developed in 1870 for sale for large residential estates, and a portion became Alms Park. The Bold Face Creek vineyards in Delhi became Embschoff Woods. John Mottier's former vineyards became the Dunham Hospital for tuberculosis patients and now Dunham Park. And the vineyards along River Road on the West Side of Cincinnati were later turned over to large industrial use, beginning with the Fleishmann Yeast factory.

Alms Park today encompasses areas in Longworth's Bald Hill vineyards where grapes, Cydonia quinces, cherries and other fruit trees grew. Plots were named after grapes Longworth tested—Alvey, Elsinboro, Crevelling, Iona, Norton, Logan and Muscadel. The street that leads into the park was once known as Wine Press Road. In 1869, when the land was appraised for the Longworth estate by William Brown of Springfield, Ohio, there were eight families living in the vineyards who had been tenants of Longworth: the Scholl, Noshang, Brandstetter, Smith, Klings, Wetmeier, Schwager and Amman families. Joseph Longworth marketed the land to his rich colleagues as affordable facilities for doing business downtown, while being able to live in the country. He was developing it into what was then called the Tuscumbia subdivision.

If Our Lady of Victory was the wine parish on the West Side, then St. Stephen Catholic Church in Columbia-Tusculum was the wine parish of the East Side. In 1867, the Germanic immigrant families of the Little

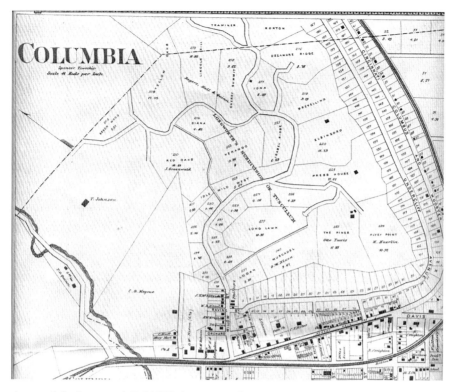

A map of the Longworth Bald Hill vineyards in Columbia-Tusculum in 1869. *Courtesy of the Public Library of Cincinnati and Hamilton County.*

Miami Valley petitioned for their own parish to avoid the trek up the hill to St. Francis de Sales in Woodburn, whose land was donated by another winemaker, Heinrich Wesjohann. Four of the seventeen founding families of St. Stephen were vineyardists of Nicholas Longworth: August Scholl, Isador Brandstetter, Jacob Feck and John Dumbacher. Frank Noshang and Felix Schutt were also early members. At the founding of the parish in 1867, some parishioners were still filling out their old or renewed vineyard lease contracts and supplying grapes to the Longworth Wine House.

A lot of two hundred square feet on Eastern Avenue was rented from Joseph Longworth, the son of their former employer, for the term of twenty years. When the Longworth Wine House closed in 1869, the former vineyardists, like those in Delhi Township on the West Side, became market gardeners. There would be several generations of intermarriages between these vineyardist families recorded in the St. Stephen Parish registers. The first child to be baptized at St. Stephen was Catherine Schutt, the daughter

THE BANKS OF THE OHIO.—MR. LONGWORTH'S VINEYARDS.

This 1858 lithograph of Longworth's Bald Hill Vineyards in Columbia-Tusculum shows that both men and women worked side by side. *Courtesy of the Public Library of Cincinnati and Hamilton County.*

of Felix and Ann Noshang Schutt. Catherine was the granddaughter of vineyardist Frank Noshang.

August Scholl (1823–1890) lived on the Fox Hollow lot in the vineyards and had moved to a farm in Linwood by 1880. He was from Rhenish Bavaria. He and his wife, Mary, had four children—Adam, Regina, George and Mary—who would have helped in the vineyard.

Frank Jacob Noshang (1809–1885) lived on the Iona section of the vineyard. He married Apollonia Gros in Gernsheim, Rhenish Bavaria, in 1835. Three of their eldest children—Katherine Schinner, Adam and Michael—were born in Germany, arriving in Cincinnati in the late 1840s. Two more children, Elizabeth and Frank Jr., were born in America. Daughter Mary married Felix Schutt, from Baden, who also worked on the land and later ran a tavern on Eastern Avenue. Frank used his Longworth earnings to buy two houses. One of those houses, on Eastern Avenue, he sold to his daughter Mary and her husband, Felix Schutt.

Isador Brandstetter (1829–1903) lived on the Salem section of the vineyards. He was born in Renchen, Baden-Wuertemburg, and came to Cincinnati in 1849 to escape the aftermath of the 1848 revolution. There are several vineyards in Renchen today, and the area is known for its sekt or sparkling wines, which create the carbon dioxide bubbles from a secondary fermentation, and secco or semi-sparkling wines, which use their own

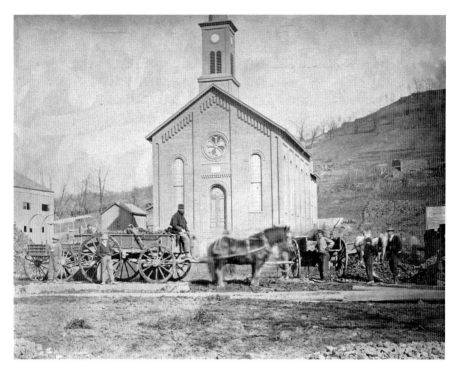

This image in front of St. Stephen Catholic Church on Eastern Avenue in Columbia-Tusculum shows Longworth's Tusculum vineyards behind. *Courtesy of St. Stephen Catholic Church.*

bubbles captured during fermentation. Sekt is very similar to the Sparkling Catawba made at the Longworth Wine House. Isador married Maria Anna Dumbacher in 1856 at St. Francis de Sales in Woodburn and had nine children, with four surviving into adulthood.

In 1869, Isador bought a ninety-nine-year lease on a nine-and-a-half-acre lot on the Franklin plot, next to where he had worked, payable $379 annually, with an option to purchase in twenty years. He eventually purchased the farm lot, which is now bounded by Tweed, Kroger and Earl's Court in Mount Lookout. At the time, Kroger was called Beechmont Avenue, and it would later be called Brandstetter Avenue. But when Barney Kroger's son Fred Kroger bought land next door, his name was more prominent and he won the street naming rights. Joseph Brandstetter married Elizabeth Noshang, daughter of vineyardist Frank Noshang, and took over his father's property in about 1905 until it was sold in 1922. He operated a sand, gravel, cinder, hauling and excavation business there. The aging Isador moved in with his son John to escape the large and young family of Joseph and Lizzy. John owned a grocery on Delta Avenue next to the Lincoln School and lived next door. Isador died there in 1905.

Jacob Schwager (1825–1881) came to Cincinnati from Baden-Wuertemburg and lived on the Norton section of the vineyard. In 1855, he married Lena Kieser at St. Paul German Evangelical Church on Race and Fifteenth Streets. They had children George; Ludwig; Charles, who was a bartender; Mary Lowenstein; and Matilda. They stayed in the nearby Linwood area after moving from the vineyard. Jacob and family are buried at the Walnut Hills German Protestant Cemetery.

Other families in the Bald Hill Vineyard included the Smiths on the Elsinboro plot, the Wetmeiers on the Lincoln Hill plot, the Klings on the Pines plot and the Ammans (a son of Longworth's very first tenant).

The Longworth wine cellars at 515 Sycamore Street downtown were leased to a Mr. Herkelbrath, who continued to make wine in the three cellars there thirty feet underground. The constant year-round temperature of fifty-

An 1880s image of the Isador Brandstetter home that once stood on a plot in Longworth's Tusculum Vineyard, now Glenshire Avenue in Mount Lookout. *Courtesy of Bob Brandstetter.*

two degrees—and the volume of one of the tanks—made it the best spot to make wine in fifty-thousand-gallon quantities. The inventory of bottled stock was sold to Balthazar Roth, the owner of our famous St. Nicholas Hotel, for his wonderful restaurant, and the remainder was sold to John D. Park, a dealer in patent medicines. It was in these cellars that Longworth had experimented making wines from numerous native grapes and made his still Catawba and Isabella wines. The Rheinstrom brothers took over in 1883 for their supply business of native wines, brandies, cordials and bitters. Then the building became the headquarters of John D. Park & Company, wholesale drug manufacturers.

In 1867, Dr. John Aston Warder, Longworth's friend and associate, visited Longworth's gardens surrounding his house, where he had performed experiments on new grape varietals. He inventoried the varietals of grapes in what he called "Longworth's School of Vines" and catalogued them and their features. Some of them were Longworth's own seedlings, and some were of unknown parentage. Some of their names indicated their parentage, but without access to Longworth's notes and diaries, it was impossible to log the origins of all of them. Warder said that Longworth had been a master of picking new seedlings but did not attempt to crossbreed different species to develop hardier intermediates, which was the method that would drive the success of the American wine industry. In fact, most of our American grapes grown today are hybrids, engineered at universities for specific qualities and for hardiness in specific growing regions.

Warder found the Albalis, the California Rosen, the California White, the Corsican, the Cuyrase of Mexico, the Delaware Seedling, the Early Lebanon (from Samuel Miller, Lebanon, Pennsylvania), the Early June, the Herbemont Seedling, the Isabella Seedling (crossed by Shakers of Union Village), the Kissam (from Orange, New Jersey, resembling the Diana), the Longworth's Monster, the Lyman, the Marion, the Marique, the Shaker Seedling (from Union Village) and the Rogers Hybrids #2, #6 and #20.

Warder said sadly in his September 15, 1867 report:

> *Mr. Longworth has been called away from his very interesting school of vines, before they had been fairly tested, and there is no one to carry on his experiments. The growth of the city demands the very spaces they occupy, and another summer may see the excavations preparatory to the erection of splendid houses, where, for thirty years, this persevering vine-student trained the canes, and led the tendrils upon his favorite grape trellises. Pioneer of Viticulture in the West, he has nobly opened the way—who will follow in it?*

After Longworth's death, the Underwood Company of Columbus continued to propagate the vines found in his vineyard and exhibited some at the 1865 Ohio State Fair.

Longworth's grandson William Polk Anderson mustered out of the army as a captain and came back to Cincinnati to run the Longworth Wine House with his brother Fredrick Pope Anderson, both of whom had no experience in winemaking or had been involved in any way in the Cincinnati Horticultural Society or the Winegrowers' Association. But William Anderson was a serial CEO who at the time was also a director at the Ohio and Pennsylvania Coal Company. So running a new business venture, especially a family one, excited him. By the end of his career, William Anderson was director of multiple companies and organizations: the Big Four and Chesapeake and Ohio Railways, the J.A. Fay & Egan Company, the Cincinnati Cold Storage Company, the Citizens' Bank, the National Insurance Company and the American Cotton Oil Company. Longworth's only son, Joseph Longworth, had moved away to his country home of Rookwood off Grandin Road in what is now Hyde Park, east of downtown, to become a gentleman farmer and philanthropist. He was more interested in raising pedigreed cattle and livestock than in tending vineyards. He even named one of his prized cattle Lady Flagg, after his Aunt Eliza Longworth Flagg, who married winemaker William J. Flagg.

William Pope Anderson managed the Longworth Wine House after his grandfather's death in 1863 and his return from the Civil War, later selling it in 1869. *Courtesy of the Public Library of Cincinnati and Hamilton County.*

While the Anderson brothers leased one of the two cellars, they integrated the cellars at Sixth and Culvert Streets above Elsinore for their operations. In 1866, the brothers released a marketing pamphlet showcasing the capabilities of the Longworth Wine House at 113 East Sixth Street that focused on the production of sparkling wines. It shows in gorgeous detail etchings of the wine press, the dry vaults, the fermentation room, the bottling room and even a romanticized view of one of Longworth's riverside vineyards. It is truthful in showing that women were as involved in the work as the men.

Frederick Pope Anderson didn't stay in the partnership after 1866. But William soldiered on, continuing to advertise for the best grapes

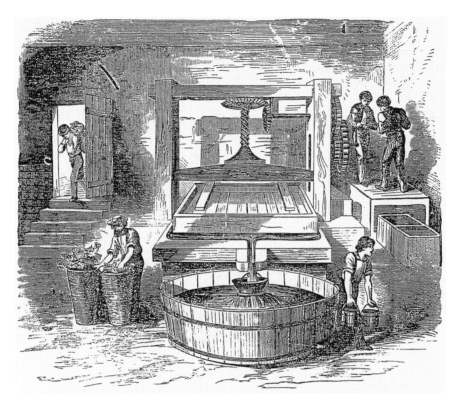

The wine press at the Sixth Street Longworth Wine House, from an 1866 pamphlet. *Courtesy of the Public Library of Cincinnati and Hamilton County.*

to make wine. William made his best efforts to improve the wine house, using the same quality assurance to choose grapes. He continued to employ about twenty men, half from France, with many having been employed for ten to fifteen years. Jules Masson was the manager. Christian Schniecke and Fournier would visit vineyards and choose the best grapes, supervising the time to pick and the actual picking. Grape growers were notorious for picking the grapes early, impatient to prevent losses due to birds, insects or rot. The imperfect grapes were even separated on site at harvest to save the time and effort to sort at the wine house.

After Anderson's uncle, William Flagg, came back from the French Exposition of 1867 with news of the new pasteurization process, Anderson installed a new heating chamber in the wine house with capacity for two thousand bottles of wine. Wine heated in accordance with Pasteur's method and exposed to the sun for four weeks improved clarity and reduced sediment in the bottle.

8. Lower Cellar—Sparkling, after Fermentation.

The lower cellar of the Sixth Street Longworth Wine House, where sparkling wine was stored after fermentation. *Courtesy of the Public Library of Cincinnati and Hamilton County.*

6. Bottling, Corking and Wiring Sparkling Wine.

Workers bottling sparkling wines at the Sixth Street Longworth Wine House. *Courtesy of the Public Library of Cincinnati and Hamilton County.*

Anderson introduced new wines in the last year of his operation that his grandfather had not made. He added grapes to the still wine list: Concord, Norton, Ives, Rentz and Taylor's Bullitt. He added to the list of sparkling wines Delaware, Ives, Norton, Concord and Rentz. For the season of 1867, the Longworth Wine House bought the entire Ives grape crop of 1,600 gallons of Colonel Isaac Waring of Indian Hill for a record-breaking $4.25 per gallon.

But William Anderson saw the difficulty in obtaining consistently good Catawba grapes, with the rot and phylloxera plagues ravaging through the Ohio Valley. And so he became a director of the John B. Lewis and Company cotton oil business, which merged with the American Cotton Oil Company, of whose Ohio branch he became president. In 1869, Anderson sold the inventory of the Longworth Wine Cellar to Balthazar Roth, the owner of the St. Nicholas Hotel, and converted a sparkling wine facility into a cotton oil factory for the American Cotton Oil Company.

With the Anderson grandsons in charge of the Longworth Wine House and a sizable inheritance received, William J. Flagg and his wife, Eliza Longworth, embarked on a three-year tour of Europe from the fall of 1866 to 1868 that resulted in his book, *Three Seasons in European Vineyards*, published in 1869. He had left his Buena Vista, Ohio vineyards in the capable hands of his live-in gardener and caretaker, William T. Sullivan. He and his wife traveled like rock stars through wine country of France, Italy, the southwestern Germanic kingdoms, Austria, Hungary and Switzerland, hosted by royalty and wine VIPs. He presented ninety samples of American wines at the Paris Exposition of 1867, where the French jurors gave honorable mention to the Sparkling Catawba varieties but no mention to any of the still wines. At the exhibition, he also saw and met Louis Pasteur, who received a gold medal for his work in finding a way to cure wine of all its diseases and keep it almost indefinitely by heating it to 122 degrees Fahrenheit. Pasteur's work in wine preceded his work in dairy pasteurization. In a brief stopover in Holland, the Flaggs were introduced to a clear spirit, new to Americans and flavored with juniper berries: gin.

Flagg said in his book, "There are those who think the day of the Catawba has gone by, but I am not one of them. Its wine has qualities which peculiarly fit it to combine with sugar, either in the bottle or in the cobbler. Americans love pop, foam, and noise and will always consume largely of gaseous drinks. They have in the Catawba a wine capable of great things." But he also warned, "The sparkling wine business is so hazardous, and the capital that must be hazarded is so large, I shrink from the responsibility of helping anyone to embark on it." He had seen the troubles that his father-in-law had upstarting the Sparkling Catawba business and all the money he sank into that.

YEATMAN AND HIS INSIDIOUS GRAPE SPEECH

As the Civil War raged on into the fall grape harvest of 1864, trouble was brewing for Cincinnati *vignerons*. It had been a terrible growing season for the Catawba. The same thing had happened before in 1846 and the 1850s—early spring frosts, rainy and humidity-induced summer rot and bug infestations of the phylloxera. Many of the German immigrant vine dressers of the area had been growing grapes for themselves and the big names like Longworth Wine House for almost thirty years. Even those who'd grown up in the industry in the Rhine had to adapt to different grapes and different growing conditions in the Ohio River Valley compared to what they were used to. They were getting tired of the blight and the unpredictability of the Catawba grape. The Isabella, which Longworth also championed, was even worse with rot. It was used to make a woman's sparkling wine because

Thomas Yeatman was one of the most prominent Catawba winemakers during the Cincinnati Catawba Craze but bashed the industry when his entire vineyard succumbed to rot in 1864. *Courtesy of the Public Library of Cincinnati and Hamilton County.*

its flavor was milder than the Catawba. But Cincinnati was right on the cusp of finding that native grape that could stand our funky river valley weather…and it wouldn't be the Catawba.

Thomas Yeatman (1805–1878) was the son of Griffin Yeatman, one of Cincinnati's pioneers, who had run the first tavern, called the Square and Compass. Thomas was one of the oldest and most experienced growers in Cincinnati. He bought land on the Ohio River in Riverside in 1831 and planted five acres of Catawba in 1846. But in 1864 he had his entire vineyard decimated by the weather. And he was embroiled. But as one of the most decorated growers, he was who the smaller growers looked up to, especially with Longworth now gone. His words held great influence among local and national growers.

Yeatman had amassed many medals for his Catawba wines. His first were silver cups from

This wine label for Yeatman's Catawba wine shows his beautiful Georgian mansion, which sat on the Ohio River in Riverside. *Courtesy of the Public Library of Cincinnati and Hamilton County.*

the Horticultural Society for his 1849 and 1850 Catawba still wines. Then, in 1851, he became internationally renowned with a medal for his Catawba wine at the London World's Fair. He added other wins at the New York World's Fair and fairs in Philadelphia, Cincinnati and other cities. Aside from Longworth's growers, he was the most decorated Catawba grower in the Greater Cincinnati region. Imagine having to hear about his trophy cabinet when visiting the vineyards.

One would hope that he would take up the mantle of positivity and help our local industry pick up and move forward. But Mr. Yeatman would not do that. If he couldn't have success, then no one in Cincinnati would. He was up for a national postmaster job anyway. He didn't really need the income of the grape anymore. And he was ready to let everyone know exactly how he felt.

So, with a venomous tone, Yeatman produced a written "treatise" on how terrible Cincinnati weather was for grape growing and read it to the Cincinnati Horticultural Society in the fall of 1864. He whined on for many pages about how it was so unprofitable as a result of our weird river climate and noted that anyone would be stupid to continue to pursue it. He did a mic-drop to a mouth-agape crowd of wealthy horticulturists and abruptly walked out of the grape scene. He became not just a Catawba-hater but a Cincinnati grape–region hater as well. His treatise went viral in a mid-nineteenth-century way by being published in several national horticultural journals. It caused a huge uproar across the nation and a virtual panic to many small local growers.

Many of the Cincinnati Catawba barons came to the industry's defense by sharing the economic records of their vineyards. A committee was formed by the Cincinnati Horticultural Society to investigate Yeatman's claims and produce numbers that would prove that Cincinnati was still a viable grape growing region. Headed by E.A. Thompson of Covington and J.E. Mottier of Delhi, they visited the local vineyards and produced a report.

What was so tempting about the Catawba was that, in good seasons, it was super-prolific—it produced an average of 400 gallons per acre and,

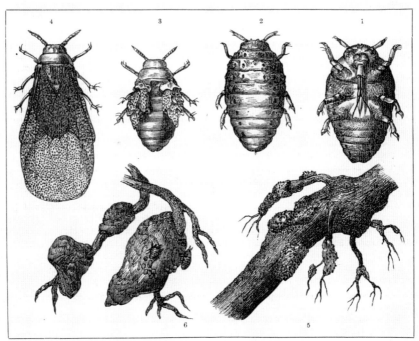

558. **Die Reblaus** (Phylloxera vastatrix).

This 1860s lithograph shows images of phylloxera bugs, which caused ruin in many Cincinnati Catawba vineyards during the Catawba Craze. *Courtesy of the author.*

in most cases, soured around 750 gallons per acre of vineyard, which was quite a bit more prolific than most American *Vitus labrusca* vines. But it was a finicky mistress. When the weather was bad, the productivity was bad. Whole vineyards could be decimated. There were other, hardier grapes being grown locally that made good wines, but they were only half as prolific as the Catawba in its good season. Meanwhile, Yeatman's vineyards were so old that all the good soil had been washed off the steep hillside off River Road. And he had gotten so cocky with his successes that he hadn't been keeping up the maintenance on the soil and the vines—he neither manured the ground nor trimmed, staked and cultivated the vines. Every good *vigneron* knows that regular vine maintenance is a must. Many years of forcing a large harvest fatigues vines and makes them less prolific in future years and more susceptible to rot and weather damage.

So, the committee headed out to the field and visited Indian Hill, where a small community of grape growers for fifteen years had been growing a variety known as the Ives grape, cultivated by a Cincinnati tailor named Henry Ives. The perhaps apocryphal story goes that he chomped on grapes while working and spit the seeds out the window. He noticed a vine that popped up in his spit radius and cultivated it; it fruited. He gave plantings to Colonel Isaac Waring and others, and they had great success with propagating it and making wine.

The committee went to the Bogens, who were growing Norton and other hardy grapes in Hartwell, and to Mottier, who was growing the Delaware in Delhi. Both Norton and Delaware were more rot resistant than the Catawba, only not quite as prolific (but still profitable). Mottier and Bogen shared their financials, which were promising and were published in the report.

The committee, determined to rebut Yeatman, presented its report at the Cincinnati Horticultural Society meeting on January 15, 1865. E.A. Thompson said that although many vineyards that past season had not been profitable, this was chiefly owing to bad cultivation. Thompson revealed that he was preparing his own vineyards to plant sixteen thousand vines that spring—six thousand Delaware, three thousand Norton, two thousand Concord, four thousand Ives and the remainder of twenty other varieties. The committee also presented data from prominent vineyardists J.E. Mottier on his Delaware grapes and Colonel Waring of Indian Hill on his Ives grapes to prove Cincinnati was still a profitable region for grape growing. They said that newer, hardier varieties like the Ives, Norton, Delaware, Concord and others were being grown successfully. They also urged growers not to give up the Catawba for the bad growing season they just experienced, as it had done well, yielding large profits, and continued to do well. The report was approved and voted to be reprinted in the daily papers.

As the saying goes, "What goes around comes around." The negative energy Yeatman put out there with his treatise saw his postmaster position voted down by Congress, and he was blacklisted from attending the horticultural society meetings. He was done with Catawba and was happy in taking everyone down with him. His words, even though refuted, had discouraged a lot of small growers, who gave up the Catawba for more reliable and predictable market garden type of crops. A large number of former Germanic vineyardists formed the Deutscher Gartner Unterstutzungs Verein (the German Gardeners Beneficial Association) to help one another out.

But had Yeatman and the handful of large growers banded together and moved into a Phase II of our winemaking era, abandoning the Catawba, and then moved across the region to growing the Norton, Ives or Delaware and pooling resources, Cincinnati might have developed into a viable winemaking market like Missouri and Lake Erie. With Longworth and other Cincy Horticultural Society members, we had developed more than thirty years of trialing, grafting and developing grapes fit for our wonky weather and developed the experience for making good native wines. We had the science, the experience and the acreage to go on. Cincinnati certainly had a corner on the sparkling native wine market.

A membership ribbon worn in parades and funerals by members of the Deutscher Gartner Unterstutzungs Verein (German Gardeners Beneficial Association). *Courtesy of the German Heritage Museum.*

But the small immigrant growers were ageing, and the next generation was more interested in city life and factory jobs. The newer immigrant waves coming to Cincinnati also were more interested in the trades than horticulture. Vineyard work was hard, grueling work and required constant care and local knowledge. And Cincinnati was becoming a booming industrial city.

The season of 1864 and Yeatman's fiery words launched the next and last phase of the Cincinnati wine industry, the "Ives Infatuation" from the mid-1860s to 1880, where primarily East Side growers grew the Ives.

The Cincinnati wine industry, however, was never able to overcome the losses caused by the Civil War and the economic changes it caused, the vine diseases on the Catawba grape and the loss of its biggest cheerleader, Nicholas Longworth. By the 1870s, the wine industry had moved north to Lake Erie, eastward to New York's Finger Lakes and even farther west to Missouri and California. Michael Werk and his sons bought interest and licensed their Golden Eagle brand wines to a winery on Lake Erie. In 1865, J. Fournier, Longworth's chief sparkling wine supervisor, moved back to Reims, France, with a snug fortune saved working for Longworth. Jules and Joseph Masson, Fournier's protégés and master sparkling winemakers, moved to Hammondsport, New York, to run the Pleasant Valley Vineyard, and even John Mottier moved to North East, Pennsylvania, to run the South Shore Winery. American winegrowers had moved from cultivating Longworth's beloved Catawba grape to the Clinton, Delaware, Ives, Norton and what would become the standard American grape flavor, the Concord.

In 1869, both California and Missouri produced more wine than Ohio, and by 1879, California was producing 183,746,304 pounds of grapes, compared to Ohio's measly 19,693,603 pounds. The Ohio River Valley had been the Rhineland of America for only thirty years. The American wine torch was being passed out of Cincinnati.

WILLIAM J. FLAGG: LONGWORTH'S DUTIFUL SON-IN-LAW

William Joseph Flagg was the son-in-law of Nicholas Longworth and a winemaker in Buena Vista, Ohio. *Courtesy of Dr. Andrew Feight.*

We must give tribute to the man who could have become the next big cheerleader of the Cincinnati wine industry, William J. Flagg, the son-in-law of Nicholas Longworth. He was involved in the Longworth Wine House and even grew his own grapes west of Cincinnati near Portsmouth, Ohio. Had Flagg taken over the wine house and continued the vineyards, the Cincinnati wine industry may have made it several more decades and perhaps into the twentieth century.

In 1851, after a year of courtship, William J. Flagg married Eliza Longworth (1809–1833), second-oldest daughter of Nicholas Longworth. He became a worthy son-in-law, agreeing to the clan life of cohabitation at Longworth's Belmont

Mansion. He shared Longworth's love of winemaking without having any experience and left his law career to become involved. Flagg was the only Longworth son-in-law who had anything to do with the wine business. John Stettinius, who married Mary Longworth, and Larz Anderson, who married Catherine Longworth, pursued their own interests. Longworth's own son, Joseph, preferred raising pedigreed livestock in the country to growing grapes. William J. Flagg has often been confused with Dr. Melzer Flagg, an unrelated Cincinnatian who was also a winemaker and active member of the Cincinnati Horticultural Society.

A year after their marriage, Flagg decided to buy land in Buena Vista, Ohio, on the line between Scioto and Adams Counties, starting with fifty acres. In a letter to an old friend, William described that land:

> *In 1852 I bought a 50 acre tract of hill land near Buena Vista, on the Ohio, through which the line runs that divides Adams and Scioto counties— bought it because I supposed there was valuable stone in it. The purchase led, step by step, to the acquisition of something over 9000 acres adjacent. I cleared off woods and planted orchards and vineyards to the extent of more than 100 acres; opened a quarry, built a tramway, until my operations culminated in a log house on a hill top, a mile east of the county line and a half mile from the river, where in different broken periods of time from 1856 to 1868, we spent about five years. I was might like being out of the world, but none the worse for that.*

Flagg designed and built a rustic cabin on their newly acquired land and named it Buckhorn Cottage because of a resemblance of deer antlers in the surrounding hills. The cabin on the Waverly Hills outside Buena Vista resembled an English cottage. It was a half mile from the Ohio River.

In 1857, William planted three vineyards of Catawbas and one of Norton at Buena Vista, which came into bearing in 1860. They continued to do well until 1864, when the black rot took about one-tenth of their fruit. The next three years were a clean sweep. In 1865, after spending $1,700 on the three vineyards, he only gathered enough fruit to produce one barrel of wine. The Nortons also succumbed to rot in 1868. William became aware of the hardiness of Norton, Concord and Ives grapes compared to the Catawba.

On his lower lands in Buena Vista, on the Lower Twin Creek, William built a stone wine house with a sunken basement, based on the same design as his father-in-law's wine house in Cincinnati. From the ground-floor entrance, workers loaded grapes into a press at the top of a large central

The wine house of William Flagg at Lower Twin Creek in Buena Vista, Ohio. *Courtesy of Dr. Andrew Feight.*

fermentation tank. The basement level below was where the wine could be emptied into barrels and bottles for aging. A small caretaker's log cabin was also built next to the wine house.

When William and Eliza returned the United States on June 4, 1868, from visiting the European vineyards, he came back quite sick and convalesced until June 24, when he returned to Buckhorn. He met with his lessee, who had wasted all the money he spent on the vineyards and gladly gave up the lease. William immediately began the sulfur cure, which he learned about on his trip, and by July he had saved his vines from the black rot. He was so proud of his findings that at the Ohio Horticultural Society meeting in Dayton, Ohio, in 1870, he invited anyone to see the effects of his sulfur cure: "Wherefore I ask you to choose from among you two good men and true, to go with me to Buckhorn and see with their own eyes the salvation which the lord hath wrought." He also treated his vineyards with bituminous shale from the area, a method he had seen done in Reims, France, while visiting his old pal Fournier, who had directed the production of Sparkling Catawba at the Longworth Wine House.

In September 1868, William visited a four-year-old vineyard in McArthur at Vinton County, Ohio, totally ravaged by rot, while the neighboring vineyard of three-year-old vines were loaded with fruit and in perfect health. That same year, the Concord grape vineyard of his neighbor in Buena Vista succumbed to the rot badly for the first time. Flagg noted that the Diana, Rogers #15, other Rogers hybrid grapes and even the Delaware had succumbed to rot.

Despite the devastation he saw in his own Buena Vista vineyards, Flagg still stood by the Catawba:

> *The Catawba, that has been made a scapegoat and abandoned as hopelessly doomed, is, in fact, remarkably hardy in resisting the disease. This has been repeatedly noted in France, where it is grown experimentally. On the Lake Islands and Lake shore in Ohio it withstood the invasion year after year, and fortunes were made from its fruit before it succumbed. If their Concords or Ives's hold out as long, I shall be surprised. In my opinion the Catawba is better proof against the attempts of the destroyer than almost any variety we have while, of those whose hardiness so many have been willing to vouch for, the toughest can only hope to be reserved for the honor of being last devoured. It better behooves our vine-dressers to examine into the disease, learn the remedy, and prepare to apply it, than hug themselves in an illusory security, or fly in a panic from one variety to another, or from one place to another.*

After a fire destroyed their cottage, William and Eliza left Buckhorn for good in 1871. He realized that growing grapes of any commercial size in the Ohio Valley was doomed to be an expensive system of fighting rot, and abandoned the operation to his caretaker, Sullivan, for New York, Cape Cod and Connecticut; he continued to write novels and invest in real estate with his wife's inheritance.

William owned his Buena Vista lands until his death in 1898 in New York City. They passed to his nephew, the prominent architect Ernest Flagg, who would own the lands until his death in 1947.

Today, the Flagg Stone Wine Cellar remains in private hands, an in-holding, surrounded by the Shawnee State Forest's Wilderness Area.

WEST SIDE GROWERS

In the history of Cincinnati winemaking, the West Side was the best side. Nicholas Longworth chose unwanted rocky land on Bold Face Creek in Delhi to start his experiments with the Cape grape. There were more acres in vines on the West Side of Cincinnati than any other area of the city during the Catawba Craze. Winegrowers in Riverside, Sedamsville, Lick Run, Trautmann Station and Delhi and Green Townships made wines and supplied grapes that made it from church altars to world fairs. German urbanites escaped the soot and crowding of downtown Cincinnati to visit wine gardens on the West Side like Metz's and Gries in Lick Run, Louis Wehrmeier in Riverside or George Fein and Valentine Miller's in Westwood. That legacy lasted very much into the twenty-first century in food traditions like Habig's Concord Grape Pie, Hubig's Ives Seedling Grape Pie and numerous local Catawba, Delaware and Ives wine cocktails. Mullane's had Catawba and Ives syrups it used in ice cream sodas, and French Bauer even had an Ives sherbet.

A wave of Germanic immigrants came to Delhi Township from 1830 to 1860. After Longworth's first experiments with the Cape grape, he started advertising for gardeners to tend his vineyards in newspapers in wine country in an area of southwest Germany in the kingdom of Baden-Wuertemburg, . That area is bounded by four cities that form the Rhine Rhombus. They are Baden-Baden in the north; Marlesheim, Alsace, in the west; Freiburg in the south; and Stuttgart in the east. Right in the center of this rhombus was the city of Schutterwald, from which

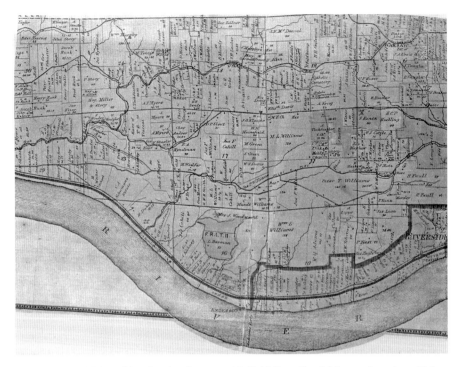

A map of Delhi Township, showing Longworth's Bold Face Creek Vineyards at the middle right. *Courtesy of the Public Library of Cincinnati and Hamilton County.*

a large Catholic microgroup of immigrants came to Delhi. This group from Schutterwald included the Oehler, Yunker, Lipps, Bross, Feist, Schnebelt, Heist and Zind families.

In 1860, the Agricultural Census area of Cheviot—which included Westwood, Lick Run and Delhi—reported 69,410 gallons of wine made by more than one hundred individual farmers. Just ten years earlier, the 1850 agricultural census for Cheviot recorded only 5,911 gallons of wine made. This shows just how much the Catawba Craze took off in the decade before the Civil War in the West Side of Cincinnati. It also shows that there was a large number of small growers who made wine for themselves, sold or bartered to others or supplied their grapes to other large winemakers like Longworth.

DELHI GROWERS

One of the oldest German Catholic parishes in Cincinnati is Our Lady of Victory in Delhi on the West Side. The parish was formed in 1842 by a group of Germanic immigrants, mostly from the Rhine, who had been meeting together for mass as early as the mid-1830s. They were tired of carting themselves down the bumpy Western Hills into the basin of downtown Cincinnati to go to the closest Catholic church on Sundays. They also wanted to hear the homily in their native tongue and have a bit more control of their parish like they did in Germany. In German, their church was *Maria zum Siege*, but she really should be called the Maria of the Catawba Grapes. This is because of the large number of German immigrant winegrowers in Delhi who were founding and early members of the parish.

The land for the second church was donated by John Gerteison (1792–1860), a vintner and winemaker who had immigrated from a wine village near Freiburg called Merdigen. His family had owned a vineyard there, but he sold his share to come to the United States in the 1820s for a better life for his wife, Catherine, and their five children. It's likely that the altar wine used by the priests at Our Lady of Victory was made by Gerteison and other winemaking members of the parish.

A fellow countryman of Gerteison's from Merdingen, Johann Barmann, and his wife, Katherine Faberin, had come to Cincinnati in 1817 and settled on a farm they bought in Price Hill. The Barmanns raised six children. Their daughter Annie married a winemaker, Joseph Brosey, from Baden-Wuertemburg, who made seven hundred gallons of wine in 1860 and two hundred in 1850. The purchase of Brosey's farm in 1847 was witnessed by August Rentz, the son of winemaker Sebastian Rentz. Johann's son Lawrence Barmann had first worked on the farm of Judge Jacob Burnet, Nicholas Longworth's law mentor. Lawrence then bought a fifty-four-acre farm in Delhi on what is now Palisades Drive, near Anderson's Ferry, within a ten-minute walk of Holabird Station on the Louisville, Cincinnati and Indianapolis Railroad. The property was listed for sale in 1888 and consisted of a frame house of six rooms and double cellar, with a springhouse, a German-style bank barn, a carriage house and a variety of good fruit trees, including strawberries, currants, pears, cherries and apples. There was no mention of a vineyard, but that would not have been a huge selling point in the 1880s, after the vine blight in the 1870s.

Protus Heckinger (1806–1880) was another immigrant from wine country who made his way to the hillsides of Delhi around Bold Face Creek. He was born in Amoltern, a wine growing village northwest of Freiburg in the Kaiserstuhl region of Baden-Wuertemburg. He came to Cincinnati early with the wave of Germanic immigrants and married Abigail Lord in June

1828. Like other poor immigrant farmers, he had a secondary occupation as a shoemaker, which he practiced downtown on Ninth Street in the 1830s until he moved the family to Delhi. By 1842, he was raising grapes on a two-acre vineyard in Delhi right next to Longworth's first vineyard. He must have been a skilled vine dresser because he was praised by Nicholas Longworth in September 1842: "There are some vineyards in the county that produced more abundant crop on the same quality of ground, as Mr. Mottier. Mr. Heckinger had the finest crop I have ever seen."

In 1846, Heckinger sold four hundred gallons of a total of one thousand gallons of juice he produced on one and a third acres of vines to Longworth for $500. That left quite an amount of juice to make wine for his family and friends. Heckinger and Abigail had eleven children, baptized at Our Lady of Victory Catholic Church, a large army of free vineyard workers. His sons must not have liked the farm life because by the time of his death in 1880, only a daughter, Sarah Jane, was living with them on the farm. His sons all had moved away or were working jobs in downtown Cincinnati.

Anthony Tuchfarber (circa 1775–1858), Longworth's first successful Catawba tenant, was also a member of Our Lady of Victory Parish. He and his wife, Maria Metzger, came to Delhi in 1833 from Niederrimsingen, Baden-Wuertemburg, with children Therese, George, Anton, Lawrence, Rubard, Rosina, Stephen, Baptiste and Grezentia. Together they farmed the ten acres of Catawba and Cape vineyards.

Ignatz Witterstaetter (1781–1849) came to the United States in 1832 with his wife, Mary Elizabeth, and at least two children, Ignatius Jr. and Mary Ann. They came from Achern, Ortenaukreis, Baden-Wuertemburg, which is due north of Freiburg and ten miles southeast of Baden-Baden. They were living on their Delhi farm by 1837, as they appear as members of Our Lady of Victory that year. They lived on twenty-two acres at the corner of Pedretti and Foley Roads. The elder Ignatz died in 1849, and Elizabeth followed around 1857. Their son Ignaz Jr., born in 1822, married Louise Kupferle and built the first greenhouse in Cincinnati. In 1869, he was listed as wine and fruit grower above Riverside. Ignatz's grandson Richard Witterstaetter started the R.C. Witterstaetter & Sons Nursery and became known as the "Carnation King."

The Martini family's interesting immigration story survives as a record of what brought many families to Cincinnati. Johannes Nicklaus Martini and his wife, Anna Grau Martini, knew that they had to do something to keep their eight children from starving. Crops in the fields in their village of Walschbronn in Lorraine, France, were rotting in 1850.

Johannes had a cousin in Cincinnati named Peter Strassel, who paid for the passage of Johannes and two of his sons, Philip, age eighteen, and John, age sixteen. The intent was to save to bring over the rest of the family. The three landed in New Orleans in 1850, traveling up the Mississippi and Ohio Rivers to Cincinnati.

They worked on the Strassel farm for about two years. Johannes had hoped to bring the rest of the family, consisting of Anne and their other six children. But he contracted malaria and went home to recover, never returning. Philip and John saved the money they made working on Strassel's farm and paid back their passage on the two-dollars-per-week salary.

Phillip Martini (1832–1925) married Magdalena Kleem from Sedamsville and settled in White Oak. Sometime after 1870, Phillip bought sixteen acres where Martini Knolls is today

A bottle of Blackberry Burgundy wine made by the Witterstaetter family, early Delhi Township winemakers and builders of its first greenhouse. *Courtesy of the Delhi Historical Society.*

and built a brick homestead to house his family of twelve children. Phillip became a truck farmer, selling his products in downtown markets. He had a vineyard of Concord grapes and diversified like many others with apple and peach orchards, strawberries and even his own tobacco. He would buy clay pipes and make the stem for them with grapevine he'd pruned from his vineyard. He also made wooden shoes for the other West Side gardeners and vintners and sold them to local saloon keepers for distribution (seventy-five cents per pair and fifty cents per pair for kids).

Theodor Gregor Lipps (1799–1879) and his wife, Elizabeth Zind (1802–1896), came to Delhi in Cincinnati in 1831 with their seven children from Schutterwald, Baden-Wuertemburg. Theodor and Elizabeth would have a total of twelve children. They originally bought a twenty-two-acre farm on Bender at Old Delhi Pike from a man named Rennert. They moved for a short time to North Vernon, Indiana, about an hour west of Cincinnati, but returned to Delhi in 1846 and bought land on Pedretti and Mount Alverno, very near Longworth's vineyards; they may even have originally been tenant farmers for Longworth. Theodor's son Andrew (1825–1909) inherited most of his land from his father, and his sons Henry (1866–1952) and Andrew Jr. (1860–1947) lived on the land at Pedretti and Mount Alverno. Theodor and Elizabeth were members of Our Lady of Victory in Delhi.

Phillip Martini, from Alsace-Lorraine, and his wife, Magdalena, grew Concord grapes and made wine in White Oak. *Courtesy of Delhi Historical Society.*

Fig. 6.—Young America Cider and Wine Mill.

This Young America model wine press used by many generations of the Lipps family was recommended in Charles Reemelin's 1868 *Wine-Maker's Guide. Courtesy of the Lipps family.*

In 1846, the year after Gregory Lipps came back to Cincy from Indiana, he was listed in Melzer Flagg's report to the Cincinnati Horticultural Society as having a one-acre vineyard bearing fruit that was affected by the frost. He did not produce any wine that year.

Their wine press is still being used to make wine and goes as far back as three generations in recent memory. The wine recipe makes a very sweet wine from Concord grapes. The recipe uses a secret family ratio of pounds of sugar to pounds of grapes. Sometimes they ferment with the skins on (a Swiss method) and sometimes not. The wine becomes less sweet as it ages. Some of the old wine is saved and used in the next batch as a starter wine, which was a procedure used by Longworth in his sparkling wines. The original recipe probably called for Catawba grapes and similar methods, indicating a connection back to the Longworth Wine House.

SEBASTIAN RENTZ: THE MUSICAL BAKER TURNED WINEMAKER

Sebastian Rentz (1799–1866) is one of the early standout German growers of the Catawba in Delhi. He is also one of the few growers who has a

Cincinnati street named in his honor. He is the only German vineyard owner who cultivated a native grape variety, the Rentz Seedling, which was sold and used widely. He bought forty acres in 1836 that would extend to Foley, Pedretti, Fehr and Virgil Roads in Delhi, and in 1840, he built a large, seventeen-room frame house with an extensive wine cellar at the corner of Foley Road and what would become Rentz Place. He married Cecelia Zoller (1807–1889) in Cincinnati in 1828. She came with her parents, Gabriel and Theresa Zoller, in 1817 from the town of Forchheim, a few miles southwest of Karlsruhe, within walking distance of the Rhine River. Gabriel Zoller's brother Johann also came that year and settled on a farm in Delhi with his family.

Rentz was born in Salgau, Baden-Wuertemburg, to a stocking maker, Eugene Rentz (1775–1840), and Elizabeth Scheffler. He apprenticed as a baker but had some serious wanderlust. He hooked up with a wealthy family and traveled with them in 1822 to Italy, where he witnessed the eruption of Mount Vesuvius. His travels took him to Mexico and then to the United States, settling in Cincinnati by 1825; there he started a small bakery in the community of Warsaw. Sebastian was also an accomplished clarinet player in the Appollonian Music Society, one of the earlier Germanic music societies in Cincinnati in 1824.

A 1970s photo of the massive Sebastian Rentz house in Delhi Township shows its deteriorated state prior to demolition. *Courtesy of Delhi Historical Society.*

Between 1849 and 1866, 150 villagers from Salgau, Rentz's home village, immigrated to America, many of them to Cincinnati. Like Longworth, Rentz set up a network of German vine dressers on his land. His brothers Ferdinand (1809–1857), Joseph (1816–1871) and Johann Michel Rentz (1807–1842) joined him in Cincinnati in 1834. Their father, Eugene Rentz, didn't make it to the United States, but an uncle, Christopher Rentz, and sister Maria Rentz Kirchoff (1813–1886) also came to Cincinnati with help from Sebastian.

Sebastian's wife's cousin, Eva Maria Zoller, married Anton Donnersburger in Cincinnati in 1824; Anton became a gardener for Nicholas Longworth through Rentz's connections.

Sebastian was able to train his Catawbas to be the most prolific in Cincinnati, producing an astonishing 1,300 gallons of wine per acre in 1846, the standing record of wine per acre for Catawba to this day. In 1856, he won the Longworth silver cup for the best Catawba wine vintage. He also grew other varieties like the Lenoir and the Guignard. By 1851, his vineyards had grown to six acres. He even experimented with seedlings and grew one that became known as the Rentz Seedling, of which he made a sparkling wine. Dr. John Aston Warder said that the Rentz grapes were a great competitor of the local Ives but ripened earlier. It was described as a vigorous grower, with large black berries and a firm, juicy pulp. It is said to be a seedling of the Catawba. The berries fell from the stem when ripe, and although it's a good grower, it was deemed better as a rootstock because of its resistance to mildew and phylloxera. As a rootstock, it thus fell out of cultivation in its own right.

Rentz had two presses at ground level in a separate building near the house and pressed juice flowed by gravity to the cellars below the residence. The cheese of pressed grapes was placed on strong slats, and the sides were made with slats that had bored holes so juice could escape from all sides, which Rentz thought was an advantage.

Sebastian died in 1866, three years after his biggest fan, Longworth, and was buried at St. Joseph Cemetery in Price Hill. He was honored by George Graham, the president of the Horticultural Society, at its June 9, 1866 meeting as one of the "first rank of those who were pioneers in establishing the valley of the Ohio as the great wine district of the United States." At the time of his wife's death in 1889, the Rentz estate was valued at $250,000 and held one hundred acres of land composing about six different plots of land.

While the Catholic parishioners of Our Lady of Victory formed the largest and most coherent group of winegrowers in Delhi, there were others.

George Vaughan (1771–1851) grew grapes in Delhi Township in what is now Price Hill on a two-acre vineyard on his fifty-acre farm. While Vaughan didn't make wine, he had gotten into the Catawba Craze and was like many who just sold his grapes in the 1840s, possibly to the Longworth Wine House. He was born in Vermont and came to Cincinnati in the 1810s, first settling in Cullom Station, then Sedamsville and then Price Hill by 1820.

Next to Vaughan was Phillip Jergens, born in Hitdorf, a village on the east bank of the Rhine River. Jergens had come to Delhi Township by the 1820s, raising grapes on a two-acre vineyard until about 1850, when he moved to Dayton to live with his daughter and son-in-law. His son, Phillip Jr., took over the farm when his parents left for Dayton. He married Maria Steffen in 1845 at Holy Trinity Church in downtown Cincinnati. Maria had come to Camp Springs, Kentucky, another wine growing area of Germanic immigrants, from the Saarland area of the Germanic kingdoms with her parents, Peter and Anna Steffen. There was no Catholic diocese of Covington until 1854, so even Kentucky families as far away as Camp Springs carted themselves to downtown Cincinnati's Holy Trinity Parish for holiday masses, which is where the Steffen and the Jergens families met. The Steffens would donate some of their farmland in Camp Springs to build St. Joseph Catholic Church to avoid the bumpy, hours-long ride to Cincinnati for Sunday mass.

Werk and Westwood Winemakers

The legacy of wine baron Michael Werk is still abundant. Werk Road is one of the major thoroughfares through the West Side of Cincinnati, extending six miles from Harrison Avenue to South Road. LaFeuille Avenue in Westwood gives homage to Werk's wife, Pauline LaFeuille. It bisects the former properties of Michael and his eldest son, Casimir Werk. Two of the three mansions built by Michael Werk's children after they received their portion of his fortune, Elsa and Willadael, are still standing as architectural monuments to Werk's entrepreneurship.

Werk's sparkling and still native wines branded Red Cross, Golden Eagle and Sunset—made of Catawba, Delaware, Ives, Isabella, Norton and Diana grapes—were as world renowned as Longworth's Sparkling Catawba. Werk made more varieties of American sparkling wines than any maker ever did. But Longworth had more money and outbuilt Werk, with a four-story wine cellar just for sparkling wines. And Longworth was more of a guerrilla marketer. Werk was one of the most successful vintners in Cincinnati and

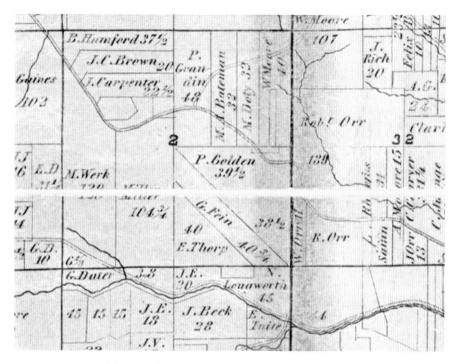

A map of Westwood showing the properties of Werk, Miller, Fein and Dater. *Courtesy of the Public Library of Cincinnati and Hamilton County.*

even contributed to the Lake Erie wine industry still flourishing today, being one of the first winemakers to grow grapes on Middle Bass Island. While Longworth fostered the Catawba in Cincinnati, Werk may be considered its savior, keeping it from total extinction by moving its cultivation to Lake Erie. His Lake Erie Island Catawbas and cuttings supplied Cincinnati winemakers into the 1960s and still supply Northern Ohio wineries today.

François Xavier Leon Jean Michel Werk (1807–1893) was born in the Bas-Rhin region of Alsace, in a town called Marlenheim, to parents Louis and Marie Werk. His father was a tax collector, and although Michel Werk was not poor, he saw greater opportunity in America. So, in 1830, with his cousin Michael Schneider, he set off for New York City. He then moved to Cincinnati in the spring of 1831, where his sister Marie Barbara Werk Verdin lived. He went into business with Barbara's husband, Nicholas Verdin, in 1832, making tallow candles and soap from the large supply of animal fat available from the numerous stockyards in Cincinnati's Porkopolis.

By 1834, he had moved and expanded his operations to a permanent location on Canal Street near Vine Street. The business was then known as

Alsatian immigrant Michael Werk operated a successful soap business while also operating a large commercial still and sparkling wine operation in Westwood and Lake Erie. *Courtesy of the Public Library of Cincinnati and Hamilton County.*

Werk & Snyder. By 1867, M. Werk & Company was thriving, with a business office located at 11 Main Street and a factory located on Poplar Street. The business continued to expand and moved to St. Bernard, fueled by its flagship brand, Tag Soap; it was eventually sold to Proctor & Gamble.

In 1843, Werk returned to Alsace, where he courted and then married Pauline LeFeuille in 1844, and they moved to the large homestead in Westwood. Here the couple had ten children, five of whom made it to adulthood to claim their large fortune and build massive homes in Westwood.

Werk started growing grapes on his sixty-acre property in Westwood in 1847 and started making wines in 1851. His next-door neighbor Valentine Miller was already making Sparkling Catawba wines, so Werk probably consulted with him as he started making his own Golden Eagle and Red Cross Sparkling Wines made of Catawba, Delaware, Diana and Isabella grapes. Werk is the only known Cincinnati winemaker to have made sparkling red wine with the local Ives grape in his Red Cross Sparkling Ives. In 1860, Werk made eleven thousand gallons of wine, the largest amount in Delhi Township. At an 1880 meeting of the American Winegrowers' Association in Cincinnati, Judge David Bailey told the group that an American admiral he dined with while he was consul to China in the 1870s served him Werk's Golden Eagle Sparkling Wine and that it was in the store of nearly every American flagship overseas.

Experiencing the blight on Cincinnati vineyards in the 1860s, Werk moved to cultivate vineyards on Lake Erie, and in 1871, along with sons Emile and Casimir, he partnered with Andrew Wehrle, a pioneer winemaker on Middle Bass Island. In 1872, they added more cellars to the winery to hold 200,000 gallons of native Lake Erie Island wine. By this time, Lake Erie was becoming a popular tourist destination, so Wehrle built a large dance hall with bowling alleys and billiard rooms above the cellars. The dance hall had tall glass windows and an expansive deck to allow vacationers to take in the amazing panoramic view of the lake. The Golden Eagle Winery by 1875 was reported to be the largest winery in the United States, producing

The extensive residence and winery operations of Michael Werk in Westwood are shown in this 1880s lithograph. *Courtesy of the Public Library of Cincinnati and Hamilton County.*

700,000 to 800,000 gallons of wine annually at its height in the 1880s. The two 16,000-gallon wooden casks in the cellars were built by coopers in Cincinnati, dismantled, shipped and then reinstalled on site. Emile Werk left the partnership in October 1874, and then Michael and Casimir sold out their half interests in April 1884 for $50,000. Today, a museum and state park stand on the former winery.

Werk's wines were widely recognized and awarded. He won the local first premium silver cups in 1854 and 1855, awarded by the Cincinnati Horticultural Society. His Sparkling Catawba was even considered superior to Longworth's Golden Anniversary Sparkling Wine when both exhibited at the Paris Exposition of 1867. At the Vienna Exhibition of 1873, his Golden Eagle sparkling wines received acclaim against former Longworth Wine House manager Jules Masson's Pleasant Valley Sparkling Wine. At the Cincinnati Industrial Exposition of 1879, Werk's wines stole the show. He received silver medals for Best Sparkling Catawba, Best Sparkling Delaware and Best Still Catawba, Norton, Concord, Ives and Delaware. And in 1880, at the annual American Winegrowers' Association Meeting in Newtown, Ohio, Werk's Golden Eagle and Red Cross wines both achieved perfect scores of 100.

In the 1860s, a case of a dozen quarts of Werk wine sold for thirteen dollars for Sparkling Catawba and seven dollars for still Catawba. Local

GREEN TOWNSHIP
NATIVE WINES

FOR SALE BY
M. WERK & CO.,
11 MAIN ST.
Cincinnati.
And at the cellars in Green Township.

I beg leave to recommend the above wines, as an agreeable and fine variety of the Sparkling and Still Catawbas of Ohio. They are steadily growing in favor on this side of the mountains, and at home bear a high reputation as wines of the very first class. They are for sale in single cases of one dozen quarts each, Sparkling at $13. Cases of two dozen pints Sparkling at $14, and the Still Catawba at $7 per dozen quarts, hock bottles. In quantities of five cases and upwards, a discount of 50 c. per case.

FRED. S. COZZENS,
Sole Agent, 73 Warren street, N. Y.

Above: The massive wine house and vaults of Wehle, Werk & Sons, shown in this 1880s image, had a beautiful view of Lake Erie on Middle Bass Island. *Courtesy of the Public Library of Cincinnati and Hamilton County.*

Left: This advertisement from Cozzens, one of Werk's suppliers in New York, shows his silver cup awards for wines of 1854 and 1855. *Courtesy of the Public Library of Cincinnati and Hamilton County.*

grocer Joseph Peebles carried Werk's Sparkling Catawba in the 1870s, distributed as far away as New York City.

Werk also served numerous community organizations in Westwood. He and other community leaders obtained a charter from the state for the Cincinnati and Westwood Railway on May 20, 1874. Werk was also among the founders of Spring Grove Cemetery and served on its board of directors from 1867 to 1871. He was an active member of the Cincinnati Horticultural Society and the American Winegrowers' Association. In 1897, Casimir Werk sold off his father's estate to Karl Kleve, who converted it to a brandy distillery capable of distilling fifteen thousand gallons annually.

Other Westwood Growers

Gilbert Dater (1818–1904) was born in Rhenish Bavaria and came to Cincinnati in 1830 with his father, Adam Dater (1782–1848), settling in the Lick Run/Westwood area. Gilbert married Louise Fein in Cincinnati in 1845 and had ten children. His first job was digging the portion of the Miami and Erie Canal on Court and Broadway. He then went into produce but made his money in pork-packing with a plant on Vine and Clifton Avenue. With the capital he made in pork, he bought a plot of land in Westwood south of Michael Werk's land to cultivate vineyards. In 1860, he made 3,000 gallons of wine on his fifty-five acres. His neighbor Martin Kreiger made 1,400 gallons, Daniel Heubert made 2,500 gallons, Jacob and Joseph Metz made 1,400 gallons together and Jacob Weiler made 700 gallons.

The farm passed to George Dater, the grandson of Gilbert Dater. He leased it during Prohibition to George Remus, and it became known as his Death Valley farm, which would become mission control for Remus's bourbon bootlegging operation. It was the site of numerous shootouts and raids during Prohibition. The farm's location was 2656 Queen City Avenue at LaFeuille, and it consisted of a two-story frame house and several old barns that dated back to Gilbert Dater's time.

Valentine Miller (1807–1876), or "French Miller," as he was known, is an elusive yet important early winemaker who had vineyards in Westwood next to Michael Werk. He had started making Sparkling Catawba wine before Longworth did. Longworth mentioned that he had consulted with Miller before embarking on his own first experiments with sparkling wine. He is listed in the censuses as coming from France.

On November 10, 1847, Miller enacted a fifteen-year vineyard lease with Albert Schmidt, giving us a rare glimpse of a local tenant lease. The farm included ten acres of the former McLane apple orchard land. Schmidt was required to plant eight hundred grapevines the first year, with stakes to be provided by Miller, and collect the grapes, deliver them to the Miller wine press and assist in juicing them. The resulting wine would be divided in half. Schmidt was also to take cuttings each year for sale, with the proceeds divided in half between them. He was also to build and maintain all perimeter fences and build a house within two years of equal dimension adjoining the current house on the property, with a walled cellar.

A difference in this lease compared to any of the Longworth vineyard leases was that if Schmidt died before the first crop of grapes was gathered, the Miller heirs would assess and compensate Schmidt's heirs for his labor and improvements on the property. If Schmidt died after the first crop, his heirs would be paid on a sliding scale for the last five years of the term of the lease. Longworth's tenants never received any credit for the improvements they made to his land.

In 1850, on 70 acres, Miller made 300 gallons of wine. In 1860, Miller made an astonishing 7,500 gallons of wine on 103 acres. He had four Germanic immigrant farmhands living on his property then: Albert Schmidt, John Schmidt, Andrew Schmidt and Anton Bunker. His neighbors Ernst Heck made 700 gallons, A. Armstrong made 198 and James Wise made 80.

Miller married Honorina Rosalie Robert (1811–1896) and had seven surviving children: Augusta, Henry, Clotilda, Edward, Celestine, George and Theodore. His eldest daughter, Augusta, twenty-one in 1850, was listed as a farmer, living with her parents, indicating that, like many of the German vineyardists, the women were as active in the field as the men. Miller was buried at Our Lady of Victory Cemetery alongside many other West Side vineyardist families—such as Martini, Gries, Baermann, Lipps and Tuchfarber. Casimir Werk bought Miller's 103-acre plot of land next to his own father's acreage.

George Fein (1797–1857), another Westwood grower, was born in Braunschweig, Saxony, hundreds of miles north of Rhine wine country. He ran Cincinnati's first German inn in the 1830s at the corner of Walnut and Liberty in Over-the-Rhine, while also running a horticultural business. Many parties and weddings were celebrated at his inn, but it burned to the ground in 1841 during a wedding reception. He then bought land in Westwood where he planted a two-acre Catawba vineyard. He also ran a wine garden where the Cincinnati Turners and several German singing societies met on Sundays to cavort while drinking Catawba wine. The 1846 horticultural report of the Cincinnati Horticultural Society noted that he produced six hundred gallons of very fine wine from his vineyards.

His farm was a diagonal forty-acre cut across Section 2 of Green County and adjoined the large Werk acreage on the north side and the Longworth fifteen-acre tract to the south. He was also close to the Gilbert Dater farm— so close that Fein's daughter Louise married Gilbert Dater, who also grew grapes and made wine with Michael Werk.

On November 1, 1846, George Fein enacted a similar but more aggressive fifteen-year vineyard lease with Bernard Schmidt for ten acres of his land adjacent to Miller's. In the first three years, Schmidt was to plant eight thousand grapevines and, once producing fruit, deliver grapes to Fein's wine press. The wine was to be split 50/50. The first spring or summer after the first harvest, Fein was to build Schmidt a house with a cellar. Bernard was allowed to pasture up to two cows and use the property not on the vineyard however he chose, except for selling any stone and subletting any portion of it.

LICK RUN GROWERS

Lick Run was settled by people like François Joseph Fries, a stonemason from Marlenheim in Alsace-Lorraine, the same hometown as Michael Werk. The largely Germanic community was made up of farmers seeking opportunity with cheap land. Longworth even complimented Lick Run as a good area for wine growing. Fries bought thirty-five acres in the late 1830s stretching from Lick Run Creek up the southern hillside of the valley. He and his wife, Maria Oehler, raised six children on their Lick Run farmstead, portions of which remained in the family for more than one hundred years. They were Catholic and members of the St. Bonaventure Church. A "J.C.A. Fries" (who may be François Joseph Fries) is listed in 1846 as having one acre of his two-acre Lick Run vineyard bearing fruit.

Much like the Fries family, Jacob and Josepha Metz were also recently arrived immigrants who were subsistence farmers, consuming what they produced on their farm and selling the surplus in public markets in Cincinnati. With plots of no more than forty acres, Lick Run Valley's farmers grew on a small scale but cultivated a broad range of fruits and vegetables more suitable to the confines of Lick Run's geography. Jacob and Joseph Metz made 1,400 gallons of wine together in 1860 on their farm.

Sebastian Thoma was an early settler and a well-known winegrower. He was born in Koenigheim, Baden, on September 19, 1826. He came to Cincinnati in 1850 and started wine growing at the north side of Lick Run

Pike, west of Quebec in a sub-community called Weaversburg. He served as a private for three months in 1864 in Company G of 149th OVI. He married Emilia Kaul in 1855 at St. Mary's Catholic Church in Over-the-Rhine and had nine children. Members of his family are buried at St. Joseph Cemetery. His grandson Sebastian W. Thoma founded Thoma Opticians in Delhi Township, which outfitted thousands of other Cincinnatians with fashionable eyeglasses.

In 1860, Thoma's next-door neighbor Nicholas Giesler (1812–1862), from Baden, and his wife, Barbara, also had a vineyard and a sizable fortune of $1,300. He died defending the Union with Company C of the Ohio Sixty-Seventh Infantry on March 23, 1862, in Kernstown, Virginia, where he is buried.

After the Civil War, two popular wine gardens began business in the Lick Run Valley. The first was Gries Wine Garden at 2291 Quebec Road at the end of John Street. John Gries opened the doors in 1865. It was billed as a great place to indulge in day drinking or an evening of relaxation close to nature. The summer garden occupied one acre of land, shaded with

JOHN J. GRIES SUMMER GARDEN.

Gries Wine Garden in Lick Run was a popular hangout for Cincinnatians. *Courtesy of the Public Library of Cincinnati and Hamilton County.*

August and Marie Zimmer in 1955 at their Oakley Winestube serving wines from Ohio grapes pressed and aged on site. *Courtesy of the Public Library of Cincinnati and Hamilton County.*

large trees and grape arbors. It also advertised meals made from ingredients grown on site, long before the farm-to-table concept became popular. It was an estate winery, with all wines made from grapes grown on site next to the wine garden. John's son, Joseph J. Gries, sold in 1920, and it became Quebec Gardens, which still operates today as a Chinese restaurant.

After Prohibition, August Zimmer, a native of Baden, purchased the Gries Wine Garden. He learned the business from his parents, who operated a winery in Baden. To expand his wine business, he sold the Lick Run location and moved it to Madison Road in Oakley in 1936. He moved it again in 1948 to a larger spot at 3355 Madison Road, where he had two cellar wine presses. He said in 1948 of the American wine market, "Wine sales are holding up because people prefer the dinner or dry wines, which this area specializes in, while wine makers in the western section of the country specializing in the dessert type of wines are experiencing a slump in sales." Gus and his wife, Marie, offered a limited menu of charcuterie with his house-made still and sparkling wines until his death in 1964. They relied on Lake Erie–grown

This postcard shows an overview of the Metz vineyards and winery in Lick Run. *Courtesy of the Public Library of Cincinnati and Hamilton County.*

grapes to produce their four thousand gallons per year. Like the site of the Gries Wine Garden, Zimmer's is now an Asian restaurant: Stone Bowl Korean, Ramen and Sushi.

The other wine garden was Metz's, founded in 1875 along Queen City Avenue. Phillip Joseph Metz (1834–1911), unrelated to Jacob and Joseph Metz of Lick Run, was born in Hanau, Bavaria, the son of a stonemason. He served four years in the Leib Regiment in Munich, married and then immigrated to the United States in 1860. He farmed in Lick Run for fifteen years, while also working as a lime burner at the local limestone quarry; they boarded immigrants at their house and then opened the wine garden. He and his wife, Louise Isren, had six children: Catherine, Marie, Genofeva, Edward, Phillip and Gustav. In addition to a large five-acre garden, there were German nine-pin bowling lanes and swings interspersed in groves of trees. Metz's Wine Garden hosted several German orchestras and concert bands for entertainment. As Metz was a member of several German societies—the Deutscher Landwehr Verein, the German Pioneer Association and the St. Aloysius Orphan Asylum—his associations created a large word-of-mouth clientele. Edward, Gustav and Marie Metz took over the operation after their father's death until Prohibition caused its closing in 1919.

RIVERSIDE GROWERS

Riverside is bookended by Bold Face Park and Embschoff Woods on the east, the Delhi hilltops to the north and Bender Mountain on the west. Before Longworth came to Bold Face Creek to start vineyards in 1823, Riverside was emerging as the exclusive neighborhood for Cincinnati's elite, who wanted country estate life to pursue agricultural interests. The earliest of these types were H.H. Duhme and Thomas Yeatman, two early members of the Cincinnati Horticultural Society. William L. Williams operated terraced vineyards at his property on Anderson Ferry Road in the 1820s and 1830s. Another grower was Matthew McWilliams, whose Greek Revival house and vincyard terraces are still standing. McWilliams sold grapevine roots to other neighbors like the Hatches and Resors, who were interested in making wine. There were also smaller growers like Leonard Giesler (1818–1875), an immigrant from Baden-Wuertemburg who set up an estate at 4132 River Road with his wife, Caroline Jung, in the 1850s.

Charles A. Schumann (1795–1858) was the most prolific and entrepreneurial of the Riverside growers. He was born on October 9, 1795, in Bayreuth, Germany, to Andreas Schumann, a teacher and Lutheran minister, and Sophia Jeanette Lang. Being a teacher's son, Charles was educated at the Christiana-Ernestium Gymnasium, where his father taught. He apprenticed at a business called Rheinhard in Weiden, as well as in Munsiedel and Nuremburg, before partnering with his brother George in Hamburg. He moved in 1823 back to Nuremburg, where he joined the Masonic Lodge.

On December 20, 1825, he married Regine Emilie Besson Von Angelon, the widow of Johann Thurn, a prosperous Nuremburg merchant, which got him his own shipping and commission business. His new wife had a daughter, Mathilde Emilie Thurn. Charles and Regine had their first son, Emil, in 1827. In 1841, they decided to come to America, but Regine died on the boat, and in a somewhat bizarre twist, Charles married his stepdaughter, Mathilde. He bought a 123-acre farm in Delhi Township on the Ohio River next to Herman Duhme's estate. Mathilde and Charles had five children together: Charles, Edward, Theodore, Louise and George.

Schumann built a large frame house on the farm, just below Mount St. Joe Catholic Seminary and school. It was a cramped house with all six of the children living together, including two of Emil's children. But having them all under one roof meant that they could all lend hands in the vineyard.

Above: The house of Charles Schumann and family sat on River Road. *Courtesy of Delhi Historical Society*.

Left: This 1870s portrait shows Charles Schuman's vineyard-working son Charles Jr. and wife, Caroline Wolpert, leaning against a grape vine. *Courtesy of Delhi Historical Society*.

Schumann understood the hard work required to start a vineyard. In his book *The Culture of the Grape*, which he published in 1845, he said, "I am aware that there are many farmers in America who find it much less troublesome to break up a fresh piece of ground on hills, with four oxen than to work in a vineyard. For my part I have quite another taste. A great deal of the labor in a vineyard can not be called hard work, it is rather entertaining and amusing." He could be a parent of today complaining about his teenager's short attention span when he said, "In some instances, particularly among our young people, I find that they are disinclined to the kind of work required in a vineyard, for the reason that it is connected with a little attention and science, which they don't like to acquire. It is what they call 'trouble, too much trouble.'"

While he experimented with European grapes, he quickly abandoned them for American grapes. He grew the Early Grape, the Catawba, Isabella and Cape in a vineyard of ten thousand vines. Schumann said that the Catawba makes a fine flavored yellow wine and the Black Cape a good red wine and that the Isabella should be raised to be sure of a crop in wet seasons. He said that drinking good home-grown wine in moderation promotes digestion and strengthens the stomach, improving health and longevity. He supported Longworth's idea that it was a temperance beverage, reducing the desire to imbibe stronger liquors.

In 1854, Schumann started making and advertising unfermented Catawba wine, which was a delight to those promoting alcoholic abstinence. It was billed as a process by which the pure juice of the Catawba grape could be bottled and preserved without fermentation or alcohol, while the delicious aroma and flavor of the grape are preserved as a safe, refreshing beverage. Schumann's discovery of making unfermented Catawba juice came more than a decade before Dr. Thomas Welch did the same thing with the Concord grape. If Schumann had been as successful in marketing his unfermented juice process as Welch would later be, we might all be drinking Schumann's Grape Juice and eating Catawba grape jelly on our PB&J sandwiches today.

A drawing of the medal that Charles Schumann was awarded at the 1851 London World Exposition for his display of Catawba wines. *Courtesy of Delhi Historical Society.*

Schumann hired chemists W.B. Chapman and E.S. Wayne in November 1853 to certify this unfermented wine, placing the following statement on the label: "This is to certify that we have chemically examined Mr. C.A. Schumann's Sweet Catawba Wine, and found the same to be the pure unfermented juice of the grape, free from any alcohol, the saccharine matter of the juice preserved in its natural state by arresting the fermentation."

Schumann exhibited samples of his still and unfermented Catawba wines at the 1851 London Exposition at the Crystal Palace. Here he won a medal for these wine specimens on exhibit at the Works of Industry of All Nations. Longworth, Yeatman, Buchanan, Corneau and Duhme from Cincinnati also exhibited their Catawba wines. When Schumann came home, he branded his wine Catawba Queen Victoria and used a positive testimonial of London physicians regarding his unfermented wine. He even sent some of this unfermented wine to P.T. Barnum, who didn't care for it. In 1852, he made a Cincinnati claret of Isabella and Cape grapes from his vineyard, which didn't take off in the market as much as his unfermented Sweet Catawba.

Schumann passed in 1858 and was memorialized by his horticultural society colleagues. His tombstone has a four-line verse in German that roughly translates, "Below this grave lies a man who taught himself the art of winemaking." Clearly he was proud of his self-learned life's work.

Twenty-two acres of the northwestern portion of the Schumann land were sold to Max Wocher (1813–1883), a wealthy merchant of surgical instruments on Plum Street, after the death of Charles. Wocher had immigrated to Cincinnati from Freiburg, Baden-Wuertemburg, and made grisly amputation sets for doctors tending to the injured of the Civil War. Adjoining farm owners Ignatz Benz and Michael German worked for Wocher, tending his vineyards. Michael German had five acres of vineyards in 1846, with three and a half in bearing, and typically made three thousand gallons of wine annually.

George Henry Trautmann (1808–1878) came to Cincinnati from Germany in 1846 with his wife, Margaret Hammerschmidt, and his young family, and they were neighbors of Schumann. He grew vegetables and wine for sale at the Cincinnati markets. The train station across from their land in South Bend was renamed Trautmann's Station in about 1870. Henry Trautmann (1834–1908), the eldest of their four sons, inherited the garden and vineyard upon the death of his father in 1878.

Louis Wehmeier (died in 1893) was the proprietor of the Farmers Hotel and beer and wine garden at Anderson Ferry in the 1870s and 1880s. He also made Catawba wine from grapes he grew on arbors in the beer gardens. The Riverside Distillery of Fleishmann and Company held its annual picnic here. Wehmeier and his wife, Amalia, raised two daughters, Ida and Caroline.

Jacob Story of Riverside was born in Germany on October 21, 1818. His widowed father, with a family of seven children, came over, arriving in Cincinnati in December 1831; in 1838, they moved to Delhi, where his father died in August 1869. In 1841, Jacob Story married Miss Saloma Hatmaker, whose parents came from Baden and settled in Indiana in 1817, coming to Cincinnati in 1826, where they took up vegetable gardening. Story bought land in Cullom Station, the bottom in 1854 and the hillside in 1859. He was listed as a vegetable garden and winegrower in the 1869 map of Riverside. Story Woods Park is a forty-acre park at 694 Pontius Drive in Delhi Township. A portion of the park rests on what used to be the Story family farm.

John Ziegel (1810–1885) grew grapes on the hillside above River Road west of Mount Echo Road and pressed his own wines. Ziegel immigrated to Cincinnati in the 1840s with his wife, Sophia Bauer (1818–1884), from the Hohenlohe area of Baden-Wuertemburg, about twenty miles northeast of Stuttgart; his main profession was cabinetmaking. But as with most immigrants from that winemaking area, he had a knowledge of vineyards and fermenting. When he died, his property was sold, and the money was divided among his five sons.

THE NORTON GRAPE DEBATE

The Norton grape is the little grape that could. It was one of the three grapes found to be more rot and bug resistant than the Catawba in southwest Ohio. Its berries and bunches are smaller than its other native grape cousins like the Catawba, Concord, Niagara and the Ives. But it's a special American native grape that, to this day, makes one of the most unique native red wines. The Norton is dark in color with big fruity flavors, firm acidity and a sweet taste that does not deliver the typical foxy flavors of native *Vitus labrusca* grapes. It is actually a hybrid of the native *Vitus aestivalis* grape. Even a very ripe Norton can exhibit high total acidity levels, which makes it unusual for a red grape. Norton produces a deep red wine with red and black mixed berry flavors, as well as earthy notes of leather and tobacco as it ages. It's largely unknown in the national and international wine scene, but local wineries like Henke in Westwoood and Meranda-Nixon in New Richmond make it from southwest Ohio–grown grapes. It is the grape that could have helped Cincinnati through the post–Civil War troubles that crashed our Catawba-based wine industry. It built the German winemaking region in and around Hermann, Missouri. And it could even be said that it is the grape that led to the development of the California wine industry. It was introduced to Missouri by smart Cincinnati Germans, who against the recommendations of Nicholas Longworth grew it to diversify from the fickle Catawba.

The origin story begins on Magnolia Farm in Richmond, Virginia, near the current site of the Virginia Commonwealth University's Siegel Center. Dr. Daniel Norton (1791–1842) was a grief-stricken and nearly suicidal physician who, after the devastating deaths in 1821 of his wife, Eliza, and newborn child, immersed himself in grape cultivation. He went into his garden and experimented by pollinating foreign grapes with wild native varieties. He experimented with multiple varieties before coming up with what would become known as the Norton. By 1822, Norton's Virginia Seedling was being listed in the prestigious catalogue of William Robert Prince of Long Island, New York. The Prince catalogues were to early Americans what the Sears catalogue was to mid-twentieth-century America. Those paying attention obtained cuttings of the Norton and started growing and making wine.

A painting of Dr. Daniel Norton, the progenitor of the Norton grape. *Courtesy of the Friends of Schokoe Hill Cemetery.*

Longworth was growing Nortons at least by 1843. His gardener and Bold Face Hill Vineyard tenant Gabriel Sleath showed bunches of Longworth's Norton's at the November 1843 meeting of the Cincinnati Horticultural Society. He was making wine by 1848 that he showed at another of the society's meetings. Another tenant, Christian Schniecke, in the Garden of Eden, made Norton wine. Longworth even named a plot in his Tusculum Bald Hill vineyards Norton, so they were possibly grown by one of his tenants in that vineyard as well.

William J. Flagg, Longworth's son-in-law, claimed his 1857 Norton vineyards in Buena Vista, Ohio, to be the first grown in the Ohio River Valley. However, George Husmann noted in his 1866 book that a Mr. Heinrichs brought the Norton to Hermann, Missouri, from cuttings he obtained in Cincinnati in 1848. So, they had been dispersed among the progressive growers in Cincinnati, looking for diversification from the Catawba. James McCullough, owner of the oldest seed nursery in Cincinnati and a member of the Cincinnati Horticultural Society, wrote, "We think the Norton's Virginia Grape the best, but very unproductive." Peter Bogen also grew the Norton and said that it never produced half as much as his Catawba. In 1863, Bogen, from one and a half acres, made five hundred gallons of Norton wine, which sold at $3 per gallon, and also sold 1,200 cuttings and roots, with a total cost of $100 for that Norton vineyard. In 1864, the same vineyard yielded $1,500 per acre for the Norton. In 1866, local physicians started prescribing the Norton and Ives wines, and Bogen sold more of his Norton wine that year than ever before.

By 1850, Longworth was discarding the Norton as a viable commercial grape option, saying that it would not make a good wine and that it was a bad bearer. Longworth was accustomed to the large, prolific grapes produced by the Catawba. His tenants were only growing what grapes he told them to grow. They had contracts specifying what he would buy, and they had no motivation to diversify with hardier grapes. And those who sold directly to Longworth but didn't rent from him also only made what they knew he would buy. He wasn't interested in buying any Norton grapes, as he did not like the flavor of the wines. Smart and experienced independent growers and winemakers had to diversify with hardier grapes like the Norton to survive. After rejecting the Norton twice, in 1863—the year of his death—Longworth wrote to Hermann, Missouri growers asking for new cuttings of it.

At a Cincinnati Horticultural Society meeting in 1860, four Cincinnati Norton wines were tested: Jacques Fournier's of the Longworth Wine House scored 90, Sebastian Rentz's scored 85, Werk's scored 80 and Schniecke's scored 90—all high scores for a wine that Longworth didn't like.

In 1868, the Longworth Wine House made both a still and sparkling Norton but sold the wine house the next year. Lucky Cincinnatians who dined at the luxurious St. Nicholas Hotel were the last to taste this now lost Cincinnati Sparkling Norton. E.A. Thompson, president of the American Winegrowers' Association, planted Norton grapes on his Latonia, Kentucky vineyard in 1865 and made wine of it in the next several years. Without the Longworth Wine House to buy Norton grapes, it would take a passionate, dedicated and well-funded grower to continue making local Norton wine.

The Norton is the grape that passed the torch of winemaking from Cincinnati to Hermann, Missouri, and then to Napa Valley, California. This happened through a prominent Germanic Missourian, George Husmann (1827–1902), the father of the Missouri wine industry. Even while Longworth bashed the Norton wine in the journals, the Germans of Missouri didn't listen to him. He had been wrong, as they found out with the Catawba and the Isabella, both of which became almost a complete failure in Missouri. Husmann himself had planted Catawba and Isabella vines on his father's Missouri farm in 1847 that he had received from Cincinnati.

Even though the Missouri Germans had no old-world experience in winemaking, as they didn't immigrate from the Rhine Rhombus, they also lacked the old-world prejudices regarding appropriate vines and cultivation techniques. Husmann criticized Cincinnati vine dressers for many things, including their use of the stake-and-bow method of training vines rather than the new trellis method with which they and European vineyardists found success. In 1844, Hermann city trustees encouraged the wine industry by offering town lots to grape growers at fifty dollars per lot, interest-free for five years. The terms were later increased to ten years to account for seasons of poor grape yields due to weather. Another thing that separated the Missouri

George Husmann was a grower of the Norton grape in Missouri and one of the fathers of the California wine industry. *Courtesy of Deutschheim State Historic Site.*

winegrowers from those in Cincinnati was the formation in 1845 of the first farm organization in the United States devoted entirely to viticulture. The purpose was to support new vintners who lacked startup capital for a vineyard. So, the organization supplied deferred-interest loans. As a result, the number of vines planted in the area had grown to about fifty thousand by 1846. Unlike Longworth's tenants, all their improvements on the land and all their profits belonged to them. They were a lot more motivated to cultivate their vineyards for success with the latest scientific findings, rather than doing what a landlord told them to do. The swell in activity led to the start in 1848 of the first Hermann Weinfest, which brought boatloads of tourists to this new wine country. Missouri's place in American wine history took off.

George Husmann settled near Hermann, Missouri, in 1840 on his father Martin Husmann's farm. Martin was a schoolmaster in Meyerburg, Hannover. He immigrated with his family in 1837 to the United States, first to Pennsylvania and then farther west to Missouri. While in Germany, Husmann's father had bought shares in the German Settlement Society of Philadelphia, which had been established to found a colony in the "Far West" where German immigrants could preserve their language and culture.

In 1847, nineteen-year-old George started his first vineyard of Catawba and Isabella grapes with cuttings he received from Cincinnati. In the spring of that year, George's future brother-in-law, Carl Teubner (1808–1851), arrived in Hermann from Saxony and purchased two hundred acres just east of town on the bluffs of the Missouri. He planted the hillside with thousands of vines he also obtained from Cincinnati and soon became one of the most successful grape growers in the region. Carl introduced the Herbemont grape from Cincinnati to Missouri with this vineyard. His nursery operation was considered the first reliable nursery in the state, and he was on his way to certain prosperity. Teubner's luck continued when he met and married Josephine Husmann, George's sister.

After his father's tragic death in 1848 at his mill, George Husmann couldn't bear staying alone on the farm, so he moved in with the newlyweds Carl and Josephine and began a two-year apprenticeship under his brother-in-law. By 1850, Teubner's vineyard was producing seven hundred gallons of wine.

But the toils of farming life were not as exciting as gold mining for Husmann. George fell under the spell of gold fever and with other Hermannites left to try to stake a claim in the California Gold Rush. After completing construction of a press house and wine cellar in 1848 for his business and a brick mansion, Carl Teubner died unexpectedly in September 1851. When George Husmann got word of his brother-in-law's death, he returned from the California gold mines and took over management of the winery operation for his sister. Then, in 1854, his beloved sister Josephine died during the cholera epidemic, and George became guardian for his young nephews, ages four and two.

Husmann published *The Cultivation of Native Grapes and Manufacture of American Wine* in 1866 after serving in the Civil War, and in 1869, he established *The American Grape Grower*, the only journal of its kind in the United States at the time.

George Husmann finally got the opportunity to bash Longworth for his badmouthing the Norton as a viable grape. The Hermann, Missouri Germans had by 1865 developed dozens of native varieties more tolerant than the Catawba. Husmann also bashed Cincinnati vine dressers who used the outdated stake-and-bow method that Charles Reemelin had recommended in his 1856 book, *The Vine Dresser's Guide*. He said that the bows crowded the whole mass of fruit and leaves together, encouraging rot and mildew. Husmann said that Cincinnati German *vignerons* were too attached to the old methods of their fatherland and not smart enough to learn from experience in America to adapt to a whole new environment.

One direct insult to Longworth, who continually trumpeted for the Catawba, was this: "The idea is absurd, and unworthy of a thinking people,

George Husmann (*far right*) and his workers at his Talcoa Vineyards in the 1880s in Napa County, California. *Courtesy of Deutschheim State Historic Site.*

that one variety [of grape] should succeed equally well or ill in such a diversity of soil and climate as we have in this broad land of ours. It is in direct conflict with the laws of vegetable physiology, as well as with common sense and experience. Yet this has been done by others who pretend to be authorities, and it shows that, more than anything else, that they have more arrogance than knowledge."

Husmann had developed his vineyard experience through grit, hard work and tragedy. Although largely self-educated, he went on to become a renowned scientist, writer and educator. Longworth bought his experience with privilege from his fortune and second-handedly on the backs of other Germanic immigrants like Fournier, Masson, Schniecke, Tuchfarber, Amman, Wolfengel and many others.

The Missouri Germans would take the gold medal of the 1873 Vienna Exposition for their Norton wine, to the absolute surprise of the European wine connoisseurs.

Husmann was appointed to the University of Missouri Board of Curators in 1870 and continued to work with grape growers. During the 1870s, he and others shipped millions of grape cuttings to France, Germany and other European countries devastated by a deadly phylloxera infestation.

Husmann's success with the Norton became so well known that he was recruited to work at the California vineyards of Talcoa Ranch in Napa Valley in 1881. The torch had been passed from Cincinnati to Missouri. But that torch soon passed from Missouri to California. The interests and attention shifted to the West Coast because Hermann moved there. Cincinnati had done well for the life of the Catawba, Missouri had done fabulously with the Norton and now California would do better still. But it all started from those first Norton vines sent to Missouri from Cincinnati.

THE IVES INFATUATION

When one drives east on Madison Road toward Camargo Road on the East Side of Cincinnati, the beautiful eastern hills hold the story of the Ives grape, one of the trio of grapes more rot and bug resistant than the Catawba. Those hills were once covered with vineyards planted with the Ives grape, the only surviving grape varietal created and cultivated here in Cincinnati that is still being made into wine. At one point, the Ives grape and its wine were something for which Cincinnati held a lot of pride. Although it has not been grown in Cincinnati for more than one hundred years, Henry Ives created a legacy that somewhat outreaches that of Nicholas Longworth's, even if its story has almost been lost to the ages. For a brief period from 1863 to the early 1880s, the Catawba Craze transitioned into the Ives Infatuation, and growing moved from vineyards on the West Side to the East Side. There were other prominent Ives growers not in the East Side like Joseph Siefert in Monfort Heights, E.A. Thomson in Covington, the Werks in Westwood and Albert Mottier in Delhi. The Catholic Benedictine Monks of the Monte Cassino winery in Covington, Kentucky, continued to make altar and table wines from its Ives vineyards until Prohibition.

The Ives grape is jet black and has a very foxy flavor similar to the Concord. It makes a good blending grape because of its deep color and also makes a good sweet or semi-sweet red wine. Heineman Winery in Put-in-Bay, Ohio, makes a sweet Ives wine from the only Ohio-grown Ives grapes, on its Put-in-Bay vineyards.

Michael Werk's Red Cross Sparkling Ives, the only known sparkling Ives wine ever made in Cincinnati, consistently scored a perfect 100 in the 1870s. Meier's winery in Silverton made both a dry Ives Burgundy and a sweet Ives. These were made from the Ives grown in its Clermont County vineyard until the mid-1970s.

By 1867, the Ives Seedling could be obtained for twenty dollars per one hundred roots, while Catawba and Isabella were a mere three dollars per one hundred from the McCullough Nursery in Cincinnati. The highest-price roots were Herbemont and Venango at twenty-five dollars per one hundred at McCullough.

In the wake of the Catawba Crash around 1863, many of the most prominent winemakers in Cincinnati had converted their vineyards to the Ives. The Cincinnati Horticultural Society promoted it as the best grape to take over the throne from King Catawba. And it could have led the second chapter in our great winemaking story. Indicative of this rise of the Ives grape, the Longworth Wine House in 1868 awarded a silver service to Lewis Finch for his Ives grapes and called it the best grape in Hamilton County. The wine made from that harvest was sampled at a meeting of the Missouri winegrowers. They described it as "a red wine, with a slightly purple tinge, very agreeable aroma, rather acid, having a taste as though made of imperfectly ripened grapes. We think this variety promises to take a position somewhat above the Concord in character."

Winemaking with the Ives was tricky. The grapes turned a bright purple on the vine in early August, deceiving their growers that they were ready to be

HISTORIC SILVER·SERVICE SHOWN

The Finch Silver Service, presented to Louis Finch, Cincinnati, in 1868, is to remain on exhibit at the Art Museum thruout March.

The silver service awarded to Lewis Finch in 1868 by the Longworth Wine House for his Ives grapes. *Courtesy of the Public Library of Cincinnati and Hamilton County.*

picked. But growers found out that they had to wait five weeks after the grapes turned purple before they could be made into good wine. Otherwise, the juice was very sour. Even with the proper time of harvesting, the wines produced a higher than normal acidity, like the Catawba and similar to the Norton.

Henry A. Ives (1807–1891), the first cultivator, was born in 1807 in New Haven, Connecticut. His father was Dr. Levi Ives, a surgeon in the Revolutionary War who founded the New Haven Medical Association. Henry's mother had been Dr. Levi Ives's second wife, and he was born into a family of six older half-siblings. His older half-brother by twenty-five years, Dr. Eli Ives, taught medicine at Yale for forty years and was a staunch supporter of natural vegetable medicines. He also founded the local Horticultural and Pomological Society. So Henry Ives grew up around science, medicine and horticulture.

But for some reason, Henry wanted none of that and became a tailor. His father died in 1826, and armed with perhaps a modest inheritance, the young Ives left for the frontier west of Cincinnati with a dream and hometown buddy Daniel Burrit, also from New Haven. They opened a tailor shop in about 1828 at 28 Pearl Street between Main and Walnut, right about the time Longworth was starting his experiments with the Catawba. Here they made fashionable clothes for the elite gentlemen of Cincinnati. The Cincinnati dandy style in the 1830s that they catered to consisted of a glossy beaver top hat, a blue swallowtail coat with brass buttons, a low-cut buff vest, a ruffled satin shirt with a high flair-out collar, wide white pantaloons and low-cut patent leather shoes.

In 1844, Henry Ives brought a basket of his new grapes to a meeting of the Cincinnati Horticultural Society: "Mr. Henry Ives of this city presented a new seedling grape raised by himself of a black color in other respects resembling the Isabella but ripens much earlier this year on the 3d August and would probably prove a better variety of more northern climates."

An apocryphal story appeared in 1904 in the *Cincinnati Enquirer* noting that Ives spit out grape seeds from the window of his tailor shop, and like Jack and his beanstalk, they grew into the vine that produced his first grapes.

After the less-than-lukewarm reception by the Cincinnati winemakers, Colonel Isaac F. Waring of Indian Hill was the only one crazy enough to ask Ives for cuttings of this new grapevine. Waring thought that at least they made a pretty berry and could be planted on arbors near his house as ornamental décor.

Colonel Isaac F. Waring's seven-acre farm and vineyard was on Brill Road east of the junction with Miami Road. He was born in the Columbia

The Colonel Waring House in Indian Hill on Waring Drive as it stands today. *Courtesy of the author.*

settlement east of Cincinnati in 1799 and received a common school education; throughout his life, he continued to study in numerous fields. Gifted with a curious mind, he was a student of natural philosophy and chemistry, as well as being a diligent horticulturist and agriculturist. At the age of sixty-nine, he acquired a printing press and began writing and publishing his own works. He wrote comments on the Bible, poems and miscellaneous collections of prose.

As a member of the Cincinnati Horticultural Society and president of the Indian Hill Horticultural Society, Waring hosted many meetings. Although his house was large enough, he preferred to entertain at his wine house, with its deep stone foundation and cellar storing vast amounts of his Ives wine. When guests would visit, he presented them with a tray of wine glasses. On the tray was one trick glass offered to any first-time visitor, who quickly learned the wine was encased in the glass. Although he had success with his vineyards, he had no children to pass them on to, and his holdings were sold and divided between his two sisters, Julian Lockwood and Rachel Coffin.

Dr. Rufus Kittredge (1783–1879) was Waring's neighbor across the street and also planted the Ives Seedling on his farm. He died in New York, and his son Benjamin (1821–1890) wasn't interested in farming, instead becoming a very successful gun dealer.

The Ives propagation story is a bit blurred after it leaves Ives's home. In early December 1868, the Cincinnati Horticultural Society reached out to Colonel Waring, Lewis Finch and Dr. Rufus Kittredge for information on its early proliferation. All three of their letters were in disagreement of the timeline, as all three claimed that they had been the one to first discover its value—each declared himself the first to make wine from it.

After Yeatman's bitter 1864 speech proclaiming Cincinnati not a fit climate for grape growing, the horticultural society toured the Indian Hill Ives vineyards of Waring, Demar and Kittredge. The report they generated was more positive publicity that Cincinnati's wine industry wasn't imploding on itself because of the Catawba crash. There were indeed other grape options to pursue, including the Delaware, the Norton and the Ives.

Colonel Waring was the only one to present his version of the Ives story in front of the Cincinnati Horticultural Society. Rufus Kittredge had moved from Indian Hill to Peekskill, New York, and Lewis Finch admitted that he was not a public speaker and asked that his letter be read instead of presenting it himself. So Waring claimed that he had been the first to cultivate the grape.

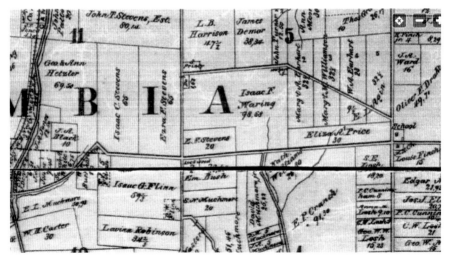

A map of Madeira showing the farms of Demar, Waring, Muchmore and Finch. *Courtesy of Madeira Historical Society.*

When Henry Ives presented his grapes to the horticultural society in 1844, he had picked them six weeks too soon, and the members of the society generally condemned the grape, wondering how grapes so beautiful could be so sour. After Ives presented those grapes, Waring said that he was the only one foolish enough to ask for cuttings. He got the cuttings, grew the vines and called the grape the Ives Madeira Seedling. Waring later dropped *Madeira* from the name, as some wondered whether it was a foreign grape.

Some years after, Dr. Kittredge came into the neighborhood and got cuttings from Colonel Waring from time to time, until he had about one-third of an acre planted with this variety; yet he noted in his letter that himself, Lewis Finch and Mr. James Demar, who lived across from Waring, were the only persons who then had any of these vines. He did not mention Colonel Waring himself, from whom he and Demar had obtained their vines. It was supposed that Dr. Kittredge failed to mention Colonel Waring because the Colonel had been instrumental in preventing the doctor from having the Ives called the Kittredge grape. Colonel Waring desired no credit for himself except for having saved the grape from extinction, as the parent vine of Henry A. Ives had died and his cuttings became the parents to all others.

James Demar (1804–1889) and his wife, Jane Rawlings Demar (1813–1902), had arrived in Cincinnati in 1828 with a family group of Jane's parents and two brothers. They heard of a quarter section of land being made available in Indian Hill by James Madeira. They moved and built their homestead in 1833, expanding it and the land on the corner of Graves and Miami Roads for their ten children. Their eldest, William, married and had seventeen children. His home was on the present Demar Road and later turned into the Indian Hill Acres Suburb.

James lent four of his vineyard-working sons to the Civil War. James, John and Isaac walked through the Section Woods to Camp Dennison to enlist. Captain James T. Demar and his brother Isaac fought in the Eighty-Third Ohio Infantry. John was wounded at Vicksburg and returned to Madeira to die. Isaac and James were fighting at Blakely, Alabama, the day of the surrender at Appomattox Courthouse. Isaac was shot in the head and died. Younger brother George later enlisted for one hundred days of service.

Waring stated that he was the first one to discover the value of the Ives grape for wine. He then resolved to plant a vineyard and, for this purpose, purchased all the cuttings for two years that Dr. Kittredge and his son had. The first wine he made from it sold for $1.75 per gallon. Subsequently, he was offered and received $4 per gallon by Mr. Arnot. The next year, it sold

Captain James T. DeMar worked in his father's Ives vineyards in Indian Hill before joining the Eighty-Eighth Ohio Volunteers during the Civil War. *Courtesy of Madisonville Historical Society.*

for $4.10 per gallon, and the fourth crop was sold to the Longworth Wine House for $4.25 per gallon. The fault, Waring said, with the manufacture of wine from the Ives by Dr. Kittredge and others was that they made the wine six weeks too soon.

Waring reported that he stumbled upon a single bunch of the grapes on the arbor where he planted his seedlings from Ives, which was thoroughly ripe, and from that he was enabled to make the wine at the proper season and to make it a success. He claimed no credit for this discovery. He said that he had done nothing for the public good in this matter. He only desired justice to the true originator. He had the grape more than fifteen years before he discovered its merit. He then went to work to reap profit out of it and succeeded to his satisfaction. Every grower of the Ives Seedling today owes every vine to the little handful of cuttings that he obtained from Mr. Ives.

Lewis Finch's story, in a letter dated December 1868, was read the next week at the horticultural society meeting as follows:

> *I leased Dr.* [Rufus] *Kittredge's son's* [Benjamin Kittridge] *farm in 1854. I planted our first Ives grapes on it in 1856. In the same year I made a small quantity of wine from Ives vines, grafted on Catawba roots, which was four years before the colonel planted his vineyard. In 1859, I made over one hundred and fifty gallons of Ives wine. My vineyard then consisted of six hundred Ives vines, planted four by eight feet, which was about half an acre. This wine was sold to Mr. Herekeirath* [probably Franz Hellfereich, a downtown wine dealer] *of the city of Cincinnati, after he had examined it in the cellar and made particular request for the same, and he sold the same at two dollars and fifty cents a gallon in a short time. My lease expired in 1861. In the same year, I planted the Ives on my own land.*
>
> *Colonel Waring planted his vineyard in 1860, from which he made his money, and his first wine in 1863 or 64 and just across the road from that of Dr. Kittredge and mine.*
>
> *Now whether Colonel Waring, after "more than fifteen years before he discovered its merits," he finally made the discovery "from a bunch he stumbled upon, which was thoroughly ripe," or from tasting of my grapes, which were thoroughly ripe, and the wine I made at sundry times, and especially in 1859, which he repeatedly did, is not for me to say. I judge no man.*

In addition to his Ives vineyard, Finch had four acres in other varieties. He had his own wine press and wine cellar that supported the large wine business he ran until his death. He was born in 1829 in Madeira and raised on his father Henry Finch's farm. At age ten, he learned the art of budding and grafting and was a student of fruit culture all his life. He was an active member of both the Cincinnati and Indian Hill Horticultural Societies and was also a successful builder for thirty years. When he died, Peebles and Sons grocery bought out the entire inventory of his wine cellar.

Although the mismatched timelines of Finch, Kittredge and Waring were never resolved, it is Waring who is given the credit for being the first to propagate the Ives. However, it was Finch who won the 1868 Longworth Wine House silver service for his grapes.

PLAINVILLE, MADISONVILLE, MADEIRA
AND INDIAN HILL IVES GROWERS

Northeast of James Demar's property was that of Joseph A. Muchmore, another Ives grower in the Madeira neighborhood. He was a partner in the grocery store at the Madeira train station and had served with the Squirrel Hunters during the Civil War. His thirty-five-and-a-half-acre property consisted of six in vineyards and ten in orchards.

Leonard Fowler (1816–1887) built a large home in 1856 at the corner of Summit and Euclid Avenues in Madeira. He was born in England in 1816 and came to Cincy in 1844, living in East Oakley before moving to Madeira. He acquired fifty-six acres around this home and planted his Ives vineyards. In addition to being a farmer, he was a turnpike contractor and served as township trustee and treasurer. Fowler Avenue is named for him, and Wallace Avenue is named after one of his sons. His land and vineyards were subdivided into the Madeira Heights subdivision in about 1900. His ghost reportedly haunts this house.

John L. Webber (1824–1878) was known as a thrifty and competent German. He cultivated twenty different varietals of grapes—including the Ives, Concord, Hartford, Catawba, Goethe, Rentz, Crotou, Salem and Wilder grapes—on his farm half a mile east of the Plainville train station. He had a four-acre vineyard and believed in the arbor system over the old stake-and-bow method practiced by the first Cincinnati Catawba growers. John was born on June 9, 1824, in Waldhamback in Rheinland-Pfalz and came to Cincinnati in 1843, working for Longworth first in his Bald Hill Vineyard in Tusculum and then in the Garden of Eden. He was a railroad contractor and bridge builder from 1858 to 1861 for the Marietta and Cincinnati Railroad. He was also a Democratic Hamilton County commissioner in the 1870s.

In August 20, 1873, a *Cincinnati Enquirer* reporter described a tour of the prominent vineyards of Plainville, Madisonville and Indian Hill. The Indian Hill Horticultural Society had invited members of the American Winegrowers' Association in Cincinnati for a visit. The group boarded the Little Miami Railroad in Cincinnati, and after a thirty-minute ride, they disembarked at the station in Plainville. They visited vineyards of Ambrose Flinn, John H. Gerard, J.S. Printz, Lewis Finch, Colonel Waring, Isaac Flinn and Louis Cornuelle. All were said to have vineyards of from three to ten acres, and all made their own wine in large quantities.

John Hays Gerard (1802–1876) had three acres of Ives, half an acre of Concord and thirteen other varieties in small lots. His father, Jonathan

Gerard, had come to Ohio from Berkley County, Virginia, in 1792, settling near Newtown, Ohio.

In 1874, prominent Ives growers included Waring, Fowler, Dr. Israel Wilson, Lewis Finch, James Doane, Louis Cornuelle, George Lindner, D. Keller, Metz, S.S. Knight, Milton, Armstrong, Jesse Printy and John L. Weber.

James Doane grew Ives, Concord and Rogers #15 grapes in 1871. He owned eighty acres on the Plainville Pike near the Marietta and Cincinnati Railroad. On the thirty-five-acre farm, he cultivated an apple orchard and what was considered one of the best vineyards in the country. The house was across from the Plainville schoolhouse and built in 1845, when he moved from Cincinnati to the country.

D. Keller was president of the Indian Hill Horticultural Society in 1871 and made his own Isabella and Delaware wine. Jesse Printy grew eight hundred vines on half an acre and also crafted his own Ives wine. Dr. Alfred Buckingham of Camp Dennison was another Ives winemaker in 1874. Isaac Flinn bought his farm after the Civil War on the corner of Miami and Indian Hill Roads. It is said that the land sold for $150 per acre due to the inflation of real estate after the war. Ambrose Flinn grew Ives on six acres. His Ives wine of 1867 was considered one of the best in the area.

The hillsides along today's Wooster Pike from Mariemont through Terrace Park and to Milford, in the Little Miami River Valley, were also terraced into vineyards by several landowners before the Civil War.

Dr. Franciscus "Franklin" Michael Metz (1813–1873) and his wife, Barbetta Reichert (1819–1884), were immigrants from Jockgrim, Landkreis Germersheim, Rheinland-Pfalz. They built a home in 1856 on a hillside north of Wooster Pike, east of the Newtown Bridge, facing a portion of the old Drake Road, which would overlook the current 50 West Brewery complex along the Little Miami. He had three sons who worked on his farm (William, Edward and Julius) and two sons who were professionals (Franklin, a druggist, and Charles, a physician and archaeologist).

They had a beautiful wildflower garden running from the road to their house that always had brilliant blooming colors from March to November. They grew the popular Germanic gooseberries and currants, and up the hillside to the rear of the house stood a watchtower overlooking the terraced vineyard. A man stationed in the tower with a rifle discouraged marauders from stealing the grapes when they were prime for making wine. Dr. Metz used the wine made from the grapes and his herb bitters to administer to sick patients bedside.

Because Metz was off traveling to patients as far away as Vera Cruz, Ohio, in Brown County, it's likely that Barbetta, with her sons and two daughters, ran the majority of the work in the vineyards, as was common among the Germanic vineyardists before the Civil War.

Franklin's son Charles Louis Metz was the archaeologist who documented one of the earliest Native American villages, called the Madisonville site.

After Franklin Metz's death in 1873, the family sold the property to the Tilghners, who also raised a vineyard from which they made and sold wine locally. A German immigrant, John Siemon, helped them with their vineyard and gardens.

Another early vineyardist in the same vicinity along today's Wooster Pike was Jacob R. Thomas. He was born in 1802 in Chester County, Pennsylvania, and came to Columbia Township in 1832, where he purchased the Wooster Pike land overlooking the "Upper Hill." He farmed for several years, planting an orchard and vineyard on the hillside. Jacob built a brick and locally quarried stone house in 1845 on the sixteen-acre site, which was purchased in 1919 by a group of Franciscan Friars of St. John the Baptist to use as a retreat house and renamed Friarhurst. It was sold in 2007 to Sonrise Community Church, which built a modern church on the site, demolishing all the historic buildings.

JACOB FECK AND CRUSADE CASTLE

Perched high on a hill above Wooster Pike and below Ault Park, at the end of Shattuc Avenue, Crusade Castle looks out over the Little Miami Valley. It has been described as a Norman fortress, and the arched stone façade in front of the old wine cellars gives it the appearance of an Italian villa in Tuscany. Jacob Feck (1813–1886), known as "Square Jaw Jake," was a native of Rhenish Bavaria in Baden-Wuertemburg. The Fecks were Catholics. Sources relate that Jacob came to Cincinnati in the 1830s and was a vintner for Nicholas Longworth. With the money he made from this work, in 1852 he and his wife, Barbara Braun, bought ten acres of land from Benjamin Stites that became Crusade Castle.

Feck built a temporary frame house and cultivated the ground, planting his vineyard. As he worked the soil, he quarried all the stone by hand that was used to make his permanent house. He planted an apple and pear orchard and built a cow barn. Seeing that the nearby Little Miami River provided ample ice during the cold season, Feck ventured into that business, forming the Linwood Ice Company. He stored the ice on straw in one half of his house cellars and had a team of four large wagons for customer delivery.

The Feck Castle, home of Jacob Feck, a vineyardist and winemaker in Tusculum. *Courtesy of the author.*

With a growing extended family, Jacob began building the large house that would become the Castle. With the stone quarried from creating his vineyards, Jacob and his family built a double cellar. The small or upper cellar was for the storage of fruits and vegetables. A narrow, winding staircase led to the large cellar, which was made of stone in the shape of a cask, extending back into the hillside. The walls were four feet thick, which kept the temperature consistent through both the summer and winter. This was a necessary condition for winemaking. The cellar was large enough for a team of horses to drive into it with a load of grapes to make the Catawba wine.

By 1860, Jacob and his wife had three young children; his sister-in-law; and laborers John Myers and Joseph Amman and his wife, Mary, living with them. Amman might have been one of Longworth's vineyard workers at his Tusculum Bald Hill Vineyard. Seeing the future, with Longworth's failing health at the time and the entanglement his estate might have with all his heirs, he may have jumped ship to work for a vineyard with a brighter future. Feck seems to have consistently had two hired hands living with them at Feck Castle. In 1880, he had Jacob Webber (who had worked for him in 1870) and Jacob Brown living with him and listed as hired hands.

Three floors containing seventeen rooms were built above these cellars, soaring high atop the hill with cast-iron railed porches on the first and second floors overlooking the valley.

The property was purchased in 1917 by Reverend Peter E. Dietz, who established a school called the American Academy of Christian Democracy. In 1923, Dietz presented the property to Monsignor Francis J.L. Beckman. One floor was remodeled for offices to serve the needs of the Catholic Students' Mission Crusade, and another floor was used by the Cincinnati Archdiocesan Laymen's Retreat League. The wine cellar, which had made Catawba wine for decades, was converted into a chapel. The Mission Crusade organization changed the name of Feck Castle to Crusade Castle, which sticks today; it is now a privately owned property.

LOUIS CORNUELLE AND DUNBAR

The story of Madisonville winemaker Louis Cornuelle is probably one of the great stories of the Cincinnati winemakers because of the workers he employed. Cornuelle was a brickmaker and winemaker who lived on the north side of Madison Road near Kenwood Road, where Mad Llama Coffee is today. He had large vineyards of probably Ives grapes, extending up the hillside along the Baltimore and Ohio railroad tracks in the Camargo Road valley almost to North Indian Hill. His brickyard was on Chandler Street, two blocks north of Madison Road. In front of the brickyard were the Cornuelle wine house, wine press and cellars. Tradition has it that the labor for both the brickyard and the vineyard brought the first influx of formerly enslaved African Americans who formed the community of

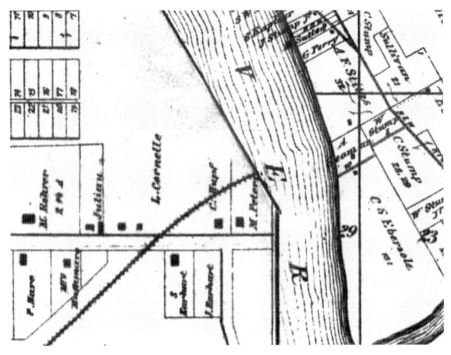

This map shows the location of the Louis Cornuelle home and Ives vineyards in Madisonville, now the site of Mad Llama Coffee. *Courtesy of Madisonville Historical Society.*

Dunbar or Corsica Hollow, which became the largest such community in Greater Cincinnati. Cornuelle was unique in all of Greater Cincinnati in his employment of African Americans rather than Germanic immigrants.

In 1959, the *Eastern Hills Journal* said of the Dunbar community that Cornuelle helped establish: "Madisonville's big Negro section [Dunbar] is a distinct asset—an orderly, law-abiding hard working people who are self sustaining and contribute much to the commercial and industrial prosperity of the place. The brickyards, wine presses and vineyards have been long gone. Of good repute, a people they brought here remain."

Cornuelle's large property and vineyards were subdivided in the 1890s and early 1910s into the Madisonville Cornuelle subdivision. Cornuelle Park, a small triangular piece of land next to the railroad tracks on his former property, is all that remains. Unfortunately, the Dunbar community has been erased by large industrial development on Red Bank Road on the site of the former Gorilla Glue headquarters.

Armstrong Chapel in Indian Hill could be called the Ives Congregation. The earliest cultivators of the Ives grape in Indian Hill and Madeira were all

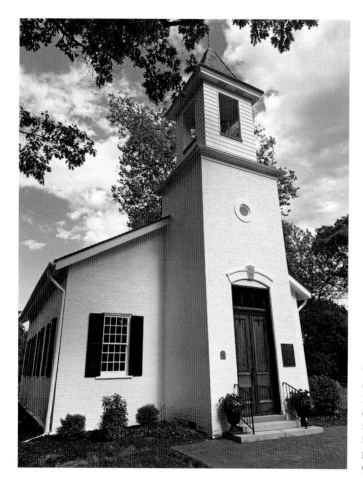

The Armstrong Chapel in Indian Hill, in whose cemetery rest many of the first Ives grape growers. *Courtesy of author.*

members and are interred at the cemetery behind the chapel. The Demar, Finch, Flinn and Printy families are some of the early growers resting there. The land for the chapel was donated in the late 1820s by Nathaniel Armstrong (1749–1840), and the chapel, built from brick fired on site in 1831, now sits on the corner of Drake and Indian Hill Roads. T.M. Armstrong, the grandson of Nathanial, became the largest landowner of his generation and cultivated vineyards. He owned the land directly across Wooster Pike from the Newtown Bridge over the Little Miami.

The beginning of the 1880s saw the last of the East Side Ives growers. An 1881 meeting of the American Winegrowers' Association noted several of the last of that breed of growers. Ernst Tillner of Plainville grew Ives and Nortons in 1881. J.S. Sheppard was a former president of the Winegrowers' Association and grew thirty-eight varieties on his vineyards near Plainville in the 1880s. Those varieties included the Rentz Seedling, first cultivated by Sebastian Rentz of Delhi; the Rogers Hybrid #5; the Perkins; the Catawba; and the Cornucopia. Colonel James S. White of Madisonville, Henry Knorr and Peter Annetz also fermented their own Ives wines.

The last estate producers of Ives wine were the Benedictine monks of Monte Cassino winery in Latonia, Kentucky, who were still making an Ives altar wine in 1917.

Uncle Joe Siefert: Cincinnati's Most Colorful Ives Grape Grower

If there were a German Page 6 of the *Cincinnati Enquirer*, "Uncle Joe" Siefert (1810–1894) would be in it every week. Joe was a big man, weighing in at more than three hundred pounds. He was a civic-minded family man who served in public office, a philanthropist and fundraiser, a joiner of clubs and organizations, a winegrower and winemaker and a hardy partier.

Joe had a connection to Longworth that no other winemaker can claim: he built Longworth's famous wine house. Although Joseph Seifert grew up in Baden-Wuertemburg wine country in the town of Ettinburg in Waldburg, about six miles from the Rhine River, he wasn't a winemaker

Joseph Siefert.

Uncle Joe Siefert was known for his Ives wine lemonade and was one of the most colorful Cincinnati Ives growers. *Courtesy of Green Township Historical Society.*

by trade. His dad had been a gunsmith but died at an early age, and Joe was apprenticed to a stonemason at age eleven. A few years later, he was drafted into the army, where he served three years before escaping to the United States. He landed in Baltimore and then trudged on foot to Cincinnati. Joe got a job as a mason, and a year later, he had his own contracting company, with more than 150 German stonemasons working for him.

We see the amazing lager cellars and beer tunnels of our city and wonder what type of men built these subterranean structures before power tools and backhoes. It was Uncle Joe and his crews of sturdy German men. Starting in 1847, Joe and his crew built some amazing structures in Cincinnati, including Nicholas

Longworth's Sparkling Wine House on Fifth Street. The extensive structure had three subbasement cellars and was four stories tall above ground.

Joe and his wife, Elizabeth Brossner, and their ten children lived in Cincinnati's Tenth Ward on Twelfth Street. But they also owned a sixty-five-acre farm in northwest Cincinnati's Germanic farm hamlet of Weisenburgh that would be renamed Monfort Heights. Many other German winegrowers, like Charles Reemelin, had a house in the city and a farm in the West Side. The Sieferts' farm was at the corner of Burnt School Road (later renamed Cheviot Road) and Lincoln Avenue. On this farm, Joe had a vineyard of Catawba, Ives, Concord and Minor's Seedling grapes and a grove of plum trees imported from Germany. When he hosted the American Winemakers Association at his Monfort Heights farm in 1871, the members commented on how healthy his vines, especially his Catawbas, looked that season. This indicates that Joe had a pretty good working knowledge of grape growing.

When Nicholas Longworth told Joe that he would give away the best farm in Cincinnati to whomever came up with a pesticide to cure mold on plum trees, Joe's son Charles, also a big man weighing in at more than three hundred pounds, began experimenting to find the cure. He spent twelve years perfecting a cure for this curculio, which included syringing the trees with a drugged liquid and dusting the foliage via a poled-sieve with superphosphate. He wrote a pamphlet about this method. But Charles would inherit the best and most prolific farm in Cincinnati anyway—his father's, which he would work on for more than sixty-five years.

Joe was famous for a cocktail he invented which he called "lemonade without water." It was a sweetened combination of lemon juice, lemon peel and his own Ives wine as the "water"; he apparently carried it around with him to events and shared it with whomever would drink it with him. Maybe this was the secret tonic for Joe's longevity, as he lived to be eighty in a time where the average lifespan of a man was much lower.

During the Civil War, when poor men were being drafted against their will, he raised $11,000 in a day to save the men in his ward who needed to work to support their families. During the Kirby Smith raid, he was captain for a local volunteer militia company. Joe was city councilman for the Tenth Ward for nine years and was an active member of St. James Catholic Church in White Oak (where he was buried), the Cincinnati Horticultural Society and the American Winegrowers' Association.

NORTHERN KENTUCKY
WINE HISTORY

The Corneau Winery and the Lincoln Connection

The Corneau and Son Winery was the earliest commercial estate winery in Northern Kentucky during the Catawba Craze. It operated in the Banklick Creek Valley in Latonia, Kentucky, a country hamlet outside the incorporated city of Covington. Jean Baptiste Toussaint Corneau (1780–1863) and his eldest son, John A. Corneau, operated the business. Their brand, Cornucopia Wines, was a cheeky play on their last name. The business operated for about a decade, from the late 1840s until the tragic early deaths of its founders in the late 1850s.

Jean Baptiste Toussaint Corneau was born in St. Iago in Tours, France, in the historic winemaking Loire Valley. He came from a multigenerational winemaking family. Tours lies on the lower edge of the Loire River between Orleans and the Atlantic Coast. The surrounding district, the traditional province of Touraine, is well known for its wines.

There is still a wine made in the Loire Valley by Jean Baptiste's family's descendants. It is grown under Domaine Paul Corneau on a twelve-hectare legacy vineyard in Pouilly sur Loire. It is made from 100 percent Sauvignon Blanc grapes and is said to exhibit crisp aromas of gooseberry, elderflower and a hint of citrus orange zest.

When Jean Baptiste left France to immigrate to America in the early 1810s, he practiced the profession of cabinetmaking, not winemaking. He settled in

An 1850s advertisement for Corneau Catawba Wines. *Author's collection.*

Philadelphia in 1803, marrying Hannah Lawrence in 1806. After she died young, he married Rebecca Antrim in 1812 and had three sons: John A. (1814–1855), Stephen Augustus (born in 1823) and Charles Sharpless (1826–1860). Shortly after his second marriage, on October 8, 1813, Jean Baptiste gave up allegiance to the king of France and declared his intent to become an American citizen.

In late 1838, the family migrated west to Springfield, Illinois, where John A. bought eighty acres of land. He met and married Rebecca Gibbs in 1837 in New Hanover, New Jersey, and had three children: Elizabeth, Charles and David.

Jean Baptiste and his eldest son were lured to Cincinnati by news of the Catawba Craze. With all the good vineyard land already taken on the Ohio side of the river, they found a hillside winery in Latonia, not far from Covington and Cincinnati. In 1851, they advertised pure, still and Sparkling Catawba wines at #2 Burnett House stores.

In the February 21, 1854 *Cincinnati Enquirer*, the Corneaus advertised their move across the street:

> *Native Wines, Sparkling Catawba (the rival of the French Champagne), Still Catawba (corresponding to the German Hock Wine), Ladies Wine (a delicious and delicate beverage) all of the Cornucopia Brand prepared by Corneau & Son, and Catawba Brandy—a new and particular article— strictly pure—for medicinal purposes unrivaled.*

The ad went on to say that their store at West Third Street was the one-stop shop for everything needed to start a vineyard and served as a human resource agency to connect vineyard workers with vineyard owners. The Corneaus even offered a bottling service from casks.

John A. Corneau's brother Charles was a pharmacist in Springfield, Illinois. With his brother-in-law, Roland Diller, he owned a shop on the

VIEW OF WINE HOUSE OF Mʳ CORNEAU & SON
LATONIA, NEAR CINCINNATIO

This shows the Corneau vineyard and winehouse. *Courtesy of the Public Library of Cincinnati and Hamilton County.*

west side of the square in downtown Springfield. Historic ledgers from the drugstore show that President Lincoln purchased medicinal brandy and wine ipecac from their drugstore. Wine ipecac, which was also probably made from the Corneau Catawba wine, was made by macerating ipecac—a rhizome—in white wine. Lincoln also took "blue mass pills" for constipation and hypochondria. He stopped taking them shortly after becoming president. But several medical researchers have argued that these pills may have contained mercury that poisoned him and led to his mood swings. Although there is no specific mention of blue mass pills in Lincoln's drugstore account, the Corneau-Diller drugstore did dispense them to others. It's conceivable that both men, who were close friends of Lincoln and fellow Whig political allies, were providing these off the books to Lincoln to preserve any suspicion of him being unfit for public office. Charles Corneau's house at 426 South Eighth Street is now located in the Lincoln Home National Historic Site.

The Corneau Wine House was featured in the November 1850 *Horticultural Review*. The article noted the increasing popularity of Catawba

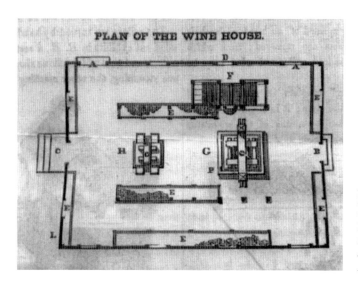

An overview of the layout of the 1850s Corneau wine house. *Courtesy of the Public Library of Cincinnati and Hamilton County.*

wine and that wines made by Corneau, Yeatman, Longworth, Buchanan and others compared favorably with the celebrated wines of the Rhine in Germany. The article went on to praise the new stemming mechanism the Corneaus employed at their wine house that allowed for pressing eighty bushels of grapes in three hours. A layout of the wine house showed tables for picking over and assorting the fruit previous to being stemmed, a stemming and crushing apparatus, a large press (capacity of one hundred bushels) and a small press (capacity of forty bushels).

Corneau's press was made by Mr. H.P. Gengembre of Paris. The press could accommodate one hundred bushels after the stems were removed, making about 400 gallons of wine, which were then transferred to two 260-gallon casks for an eight-week fermentation, after which a second fermentation took place. After a year of cask aging, the wine was bottled.

The *Cincinnati Gazette* detailed the grape harvest of 1849 in Covington and noted that Corneau's five-acre vineyard at Sanford Place on Banklick Creek made 1,000 gallons of wine. Dr. Mosher, of Latonia, had an acre and a half of vines and made 300 gallons of Catawba wine. A Mr. Jones, with a one-acre vineyard, made 300 gallons of wine. J.D. Park, about three miles from Covington, had three acres in bearing, making 150 gallons of wine. Park hired a Mr. McConnell to supervise his vineyards and winemaking. All the Latonia winemakers had southerly facing vines.

John Park bought out the inventory of the Corneau Winery when John A. died in 1855 and his father Jean Baptiste moved back to Illinois. Park was a member of the Cincinnati Horticultural Society and would also be one

The Corneau grape stemmer, shown here, was considered the height of winemaking technology in the 1850s. *Courtesy of the Public Library of Cincinnati and Hamilton County.*

of the largest dealers of local wine made by others. He was a distributor for Carl Schumann's wines made in Riverside in Cincinnati's West Side.

Dr. Stephen Mosher (1793–1864) was born in Poplar Ridge, Cayuga County, New York, into a Quaker family. After graduating from the New York Medical College in 1812, he married Hannah Johnston Weber and practiced medicine for several years. In 1834, during the New York cholera epidemic, he came up with a famous tonic cure consisting of opium, camphor, rhubarb, capsicum and peppermint, which became known as the Sun Cure for Cholera. In 1839, looking for a more temperate climate for his health, he relocated to Covington, Kentucky—he was on the way to Florida but decided to stay in Covington. In the spring of 1843, he exchanged his drugstore for a resort called Latonia Springs, a hotel with natural springs then owned by Henry Starr. Mosher was also a founding member of the Cincinnati Horticultural Society that same year. He renovated the dilapidated Latonia Springs property; enclosed the springs; added a vineyard, an orchard, a bar, a dance hall and a wine cellar; and created a resort that drew many visitors. He died in 1864, and his son, William, sold the property in 1865 to Frank Rothert.

EGBERT ABIEL THOMPSON AND HIS HILLSIDE WINERY

On the top of Buena Vista Hill or Prospect Hill in Latonia lies a rich wine history as deep as Cincinnati's. The property served as a winery from 1858 to 1922. Then, from 1922 to 1953, it operated as a grape juice and table grape producer. For about three to five years, Mark Schmidt, owner of Monte Cassino Bed & Breakfast, grew grapes and made wine on part of the former property. So, for nearly one hundred years, Buena Vista Hill has provided locally grown grapes. It's been inhabited by Native Americans, Benedictine monks, Union soldiers and vineyardists.

The first winery was that of Egbert Abiel Thompson (1814–1879). Thompson was born in 1814 in Bethlehem, Connecticut, to a family of some wealth. He entered Yale Law School in 1839 and met and married Caroline A. Smith. Upon his graduation, the young couple moved to Quincy, Illinois, where he practiced law and edited a newspaper. They moved in 1847 to Cincinnati, where he continued his law practice. But in 1858, he abandoned law and purchased four lots in Covington on Buena Vista Hill totaling thirty-seven and a half acres for $6,937. After Nicholas Longworth passed away, Thompson became his successor as protector of the Cincinnati wine industry and president of the Cincinnati Horticultural Society.

Thompson wasted no time planting a vineyard and making wine. But in September 1862, General Wright took over Thompson's house and grounds and made it his headquarters for what was named Fort Henry to defend Covington from what was feared to be an impending invasion by Confederate troops.

Several hundred Union soldiers set up camp on Thompson's property. As it turned out, the Confederate invasion never happened. So there were a lot of idle soldiers with a lot of leisure time for drinking and other boisterous activities. Thompson made a claim to the U.S. government that the Union soldiers burned wood from his fences; destroyed his peach, pear and cherry trees and vineyard; and damaged other property to the amount of $7,500. The U.S. government determined that his claims were exorbitant and reduced his reimbursement to $2,450.

The March 17, 1869 *Cincinnati Commercial* noted that Thompson was producing five to seven hundred gallons of Ives and about one thousand gallons of Concord wine. He intended to root up all of his Catawba and replace it with other varietals.

At the February 12, 1872 meeting, the association voted a resolution:

> *That we cordially endorse the position of our president, E.A. Thompson Esq whose indefatigable efforts and unexampled success have made him the first of American wine growers that the numerous varieties of wines offered by him at this meeting, in the aggregate have never been equaled and that we are proud to hail him as was done upon another occasion, and by another assemblage, the well earned title of* The Wine King *of America.*

At the meeting, Thompson showcased his exceptional variety of wines: still Catawba 1870, Herbemont 1871, White Concord 1870, Norton 1870, Ives 1871, Sparkling Catawba 1871, Ruby Sparkling of 1869 and grape and peach brandy. All were branded Thompson Hillside Wines. Thompson said that the Concord rots more or less everywhere it grows but that the Ives is not as susceptible to rot. He also grew the Harford Profile, Iona, Clinton, Delaware and Concord varietals.

Mr. Thompson was noted for his notion that vines do not grow well in standing water and that all excess water must be removed from the vineyard. He created an extensive drainage system leading from the vineyard terraces to a retaining pond on his premises, a portion of which still exists.

Starting in 1867, it seems that Thompson was trying to gain capital to pay off debts. He started a series of mortgage transfers on the winery property, selling to his own Cincinnati Wine Company in 1871 for $90,000. The Cincinnati Wine Company then sold the land to the American Life Insurance Company of Philadelphia in late 1871 for $20,000. These deed transfers gained the notice of the Kenton County Chancery Court, and Thompson was sued on the grounds that these were fraudulent transfers meant to cover up his debts. The case continued until 1876, and the mortgage to the American Life Insurance Company was deemed valid for its sale to the next owners, the Benedictine Order of Covington.

Thompson was in a destitute financial situation and might have had to claim bankruptcy. He fled town and died in Hutchinson, Kansas, on February 4, 1879. He was brought back to Cincinnati and buried at Spring Grove Cemetery on a lot without even a gravestone.

MONTE CASSINO: BENEDICTINE MONKS MAKE LOCAL WINE ON BUENA VISTA HILL

Thompson's misfortune became an opportunity for the Benedictines of Pennsylvania. In 1877, Archabbot Boniface Wimmer, head of St. Vincent's Benedictine Monastery in Latrobe, Pennsylvania, was in a quandary. He could not find wine made to the strict purity regulations of canon law. At the time, most wineries, especially those in Cincinnati, were adding sugar to the fermentation and, in some cases, fortifying wines with brandy, which was prohibited by church regulations. He had been sent to the United States by King Ludwig of Bavaria to build the Benedictine Catholic order to accommodate the large number of Germanic immigrants to America.

Catholics believe that through a process called transubstantiation, the altar wine and the bread or host actually become the physical blood and body of Christ during the priest's Eucharistic blessing. Catholic altar wine had to be pure, made from only grapes, naturally fermented and without anything artificial added. If no one was good enough to make altar wine, then Archabbot Boniface would just have to do it himself. So, he bought Thompson's former winery to make and supply altar wine for his abbey and the Benedictine parishes throughout the country. He named it Monte Cassino, after the order's first monastery in Italy.

The archabbot chose his own nephew, Father Luke Wimmer, to be the first supervisor of Monte Cassino. Father Luke had come over from Bavaria originally to run the art school at St. Vincent Monastery in Latrobe and was already in Covington, serving as temporary pastor at St. Joseph Church after the former pastor, Father Aemilian, withdrew from the parish in 1875.

The Benedictines had been invited to Covington in 1855 by Bishop George A. Carrell to care for the growing German parish of St. Joseph. By the fall of 1877, a monastery building was under construction on Prospect Hill. Monte Cassino was considered a mission under the authority of the St. Joseph Priory in Covington.

Without any winemaking experience, Father Wimmer took on the job and served the longest of all superiors there. Luckily, the Benedictines could rely on the vineyards and drainage system that Thompson had already installed. But that didn't mean there wasn't hard work ahead. They would have to learn the techniques required for each grape varietal and learn how to make good wine. Neither was an easy task for newcomers.

In a letter to St. Vincent's in 1884, Father Luke lamented, "I was the man who built it [the winery], but could not consume." He also talked about an

The monks' quarters at the Monte Cassino Winery. *Courtesy of Archives of St. Vincent Archabbey.*

interesting new grape, called the Elvira, which does better than the Catawba in being rot resistant. Elvira is an American hybrid grape with medium-sized green berries and is used to produce blended white wines. Father Luke may have heard about the grape from the Benedictines in Atkinson, Kansas, near Hermann, Missouri, where the German winegrowers were having success with the Elvira. The fact that he was investigating grape varietals shows his engagement in the operation.

During its early history, Monte Cassino produced about 5,000 gallons of wine each year. Only about 500 to 600 gallons of that wine made it to St. Vincent's. The first pressing of the grapes was used to produce altar wine, and the second and third pressings were used to produce table wine under the label Red Rose Wine. From 1905 to 1918, the winery bought on average thirteen tons of grapes from other vineyards but made about 1,500 gallons from grapes on site. The majority of the business of Monte Cassino was for table wine outside of the church.

A parade of other superiors followed Father Luke Wimmer, OSB (1877–88): Father Alphonse Heimler, OSB (1888); Father Paulinus Wenkmann, OSB (1888); Father Sebastian Arnold, OSB (1888–1894 and 1908–10);

Benedictine Superiors of Monte Casino Winery.

The Rev. Luke Wimmer
1877–1888

Rev. Alphonse Heimler
1888

Abbot Boniface Wimmer,
OF St. Vincent Abbey;
Latrobe, PA,
Founding Abbot of
Monte Casino Winery

Rev. Paulinus Wenkmann
1888

Rev. Sebastian Arnold
1888–1894; 1908–1910

REV. OTTO KOPF.
1894–1908

Rev. Modestus Wirtner
1910–1919

Rev. Celestine Huber   1919–1925

The Benedictine priests who oversaw the operations of Monte Cassino Winery. *Courtesy of the Archives of St. Vincent Archabbey.*

Father Otto Kopf, OSB (1894–1908); Father Modestus Wirtner, OSB (1910–19); and finally Father Celestine Huber, OSB (1919–22).

Father Alphonse became supervisor of Monte Cassino after Father Luke but only lasted a few months, not even to the harvest and winemaking in September/October. Then Father Paulinus Wenckmann came and then Father Sebastian Arnold, who lasted until 1894, the year he built the new wine house and left the winery with a reduced state of capital.

In October 1888, Father Paulinus Wenckmann oversaw the winemaking before leaving. He reported that the monks made 900 gallons of Concord, 2,600 gallons of Ives, 450 gallons of Black Rose, 450 gallons of Riesling and Elvira and 500 gallons of Catawba and Diana.

By 1894, the fragility of the business at Monte Cassino was seen in a letter from Father Otto Kopf to the abbot at St. Vincent:

> *I received your letter of October fifth. unfortunately i have no work for the son of Baron von Cetto, not that we do not have any work, but none for such wages can be given as the baron's son wished and received at St. Vincent. Only the driver gets $15 the other driver gets $13 a month and both are good mannered and known for their business. The cellar master Theobald Weiss gets $30 while the others only earn 8 and 5 dollars a month. I had to send away three workers that I needed very badly and each of whom*

received $4.50 per night because the business is too bad and the expenses are too high.

By 1917, the vines were fatigued and producing less fruit. Father Modestus Wirtner complained of another problem: "When bought in 1877 the place was in the country now a part is within the city limits—yet we have no city protection, no police, no fire protection, no city light, no city water—only city tax and a lot of city thieves and city rabbit hunters who tear down walls [in the vineyard] and shutter buildings to catch the rabbits." The City of Covington taxed the wine house and cellar, with the justification being that it benefited from being in the incorporated part of the city.

The winery consisted of a main twenty-eight-by-sixty-seven-foot stone building with one story above ground and two stories below. This had been built during Father Sebastian's time, when the original timber-frame Thompson wine building was torn down and replaced with a stronger structure. An adjoining twenty-eight-by-fifty-foot in-ground cellar was built during Father Otto Kopf's time. A one-ton grape press was in the front part of the winery complex, and ten wooden fermentation vats sat in the press room. These expansions indicate a growing wine business toward the turn of the nineteenth century. At its height, three monks handled the wagon wine delivery business to Covington and surrounding areas. Three to four monks were in charge of tending the vineyards, and several others were in charge of the winemaking operations. In addition to the two-story brick monastery and the winemaking buildings, there were also a frame carpenter shop, a blacksmith shop, a wagon shed, a barn and a two-story brick workman's dormitory.

The most unusual building on the monastery site was a small fieldstone chapel dedicated to Mary the "Sorrowful Mother." This chapel was built by Brother Albert Soltis, OSB, under the direction of then superior Father Otto Kopf around 1904. The interior of the building measured six by nine feet and could only hold about three monks at a time. The centerpiece of the chapel was a statue of the *Pietà*. Over the door was inscribed in the German language *Sehet ob ein schmerz Meiningen gleiche*, which means, "There is no sorrow like my sorrow." The chapel stood just in front of the house overlooking the vines.

An account by superior Father Modestus Wirtner in his last year, 1917, gives us the breakdown of wines made and sold at Monte Cassino. The vineyard produced a harvest of 32,637 pounds of grapes. The Delaware grapes were offered at $110 per ton but were not sold. A total of 6,835

This 1894 photograph shows workers in front of the new Monte Cassino Winehouse during Father Sebastian Arnold's leadership. *Courtesy of Archives of St. Vincent Archabbey.*

gallons of wine—710 gallons of Riesling altar wine and 6,125 gallons of table wine—was made in 1917. These were made from California-purchased grapes. Presumably the second and third Riesling presses made no more than 1,420 gallons of table wine, and the rest would have been made from the Delaware grapes, which would have made the Black Rose label wine.

A total of 10,227.5 gallons of altar wine and table wine was sold. Of the 1,266 gallons of altar wine sold, nearly half—600 gallons (400 gallons of Riesling and 200 gallons of Ives)—was sold to St. Vincent. The remainder of altar wine sold, 400 gallons, was its Black Rose. So only 10 percent of the wine operation of Monte Cassino was for altar wines, with the majority being table wines for private consumption. This means that the success of the operation was due to success of sales of non-church wine to private consumers. And that all came to a crash when Prohibition came.

During Prohibition, Monte Cassino became Bonded Winery #1, only allowed to make altar wine up to 1,000 gallons annually, a significant decrease from its normal 5,000 gallons. After Father Modestus Wirtner got his wish and left his position of superior, Father Celestine Huber, who had been assistant

Looking out over the Monte Cassino vineyards. *Courtesy of Archives of St. Vincent Archabbey.*

View into the Monte Cassino complex, with vineyards on the left. *Courtesy of Archives of St. Vincent Archabbey.*

pastor at St. Joseph's since 1913, became the government-approved agent, a sort of priestly George Remus. He oversaw the depletion of all the now government-bonded wine in storage at the Monte Cassino wine cellar, after all winemaking operations were shut down. In 1919, during Prohibition, 500 gallons of Black Rose Altar Wine were sent to St. Vincent and 800 gallons of total altar wine were made, but the total business lost $1,500. In 1920, 1,376 gallons of altar wine were made, and the operations lost $1,000. In 1922, $1,000 was made from sale of altar wines—about 870 gallons.

Huber reported back to St. Vincent in 1919 that only 196 gallons of altar wine existed in the cellars. He also noted that they had the ability to buy seven thousand pounds of Norton grapes from Father Hillemeyer, as Father Modestus had done the previous year. The brothers at this unnamed winery had almost pulled up the Nortons to make room to plant tobacco, as they thought Prohibition would yield the Norton grapevines useless. This may have been the last wine produced at Monte Cassino. The last monks left the property in 1922. Many were saddened when Father Huber left St. Joseph's in 1925 for St. Mary's Parish in North Side, Pittsburgh.

A group photo of the last monks who worked at Monte Cassino. *Courtesy of the Archives of St. Vincent Archabbey.*

In 1922, the last winemaking monk on site was Brother Placidus Maier, an immigrant from Bordensee, a little town on the German side of the Swiss Alps. He was the last to attend to the thirty acres of vineyards, doing the job of four men. He had come to Monte Cassino in 1919 to help tend the Concord, Hartford, Ives, Catawba, Delaware and Norton grapes, as well as to make the wine.

When the monks ceased operations, they leased the property to Frank Burkhardt from 1922 to 1953. His family made unfermented grape juice, which they sold along with the grapes to locals. What the customer did with the grape juice after they bought it was their business. The Burkhardts also operated as a poultry farm, selling cooking and hatching eggs and pure-bred baby chicks. At Easter, they did a large business selling colored Easter eggs to parishioners of St. Joseph's.

The Monte Cassino property was sold to Fred Riedinger in 1957. Riedinger then sold the property (except for the little chapel) to Hanser Homes Inc. in 1960. It built a subdivision on the property, naming two of the subdivision's streets Monte and Casino to pay tribute to the old monastery.

In the 1950s and 1960s, the Greenburg family on Caroline Street in Latonia formed the Monte Cassino Wine Company. Riding on the coattails of the Monte Cassino wines, they sold Muscatel and White Port Wine made from California grapes in elegant violin-shaped and glass cork–topped flasks and bottles.

Fred Riedinger donated the little chapel to Thomas More College in memory of his deceased mother, Alma. On April 7, 1965, the little chapel was moved from its original location by flatbed truck six miles to the Thomas More campus. The trip took five hours to complete. The chapel was placed on new foundations facing a lake near the entrance to the college. This is the last remnant of the Monte Cassino Winery.

In 1999, Mark Schmidt bought an old hillside property in Latonia, surrounding the 1830s house of Father Ferdinand Kuhr, the first pastor of Mother of God Parish. Although Schmidt knew none of the winemaking history on Buena Vista Hill, he had wine in his DNA. He grew up next to the Meier's Winery in Deer Park, and his printing business, Studio Vertu, was printing wine label coasters for wineries across the country.

An advertisement for Monte Cassino grapes when the Burkhardt family were renting the property. *Courtesy of Kenton County Library.*

The world's smallest chapel, built by Brother Albert Soltis under the direction of Father Otto Kopf. *Courtesy of Archives of St. Vincent Archabbey.*

Mark found the old stone terraces and network of irrigation gutters that led to a reservoir. He found out that his hilltop property was the farthest edge of the old Monte Cassino Winery. With a recommendation from Larry Leep, head of the Kentucky Wine Growers Association, Mark decided to plant and grow the Dornfelder grape from Germany on these terraces. The vines produced grapes, but he soon learned the same pitfalls of grape growing as Cincinnati Catawba growers of old. The first year, the birds got the grapes. The second year, he put netting around the vines, but the raccoons got them. Then the deer. Then in the fourth year a disease infested the vines. Schmidt said that he should have just buried his retirement money in a ditch and accomplished the same as all the money he spent on the vineyard. In his first night's rental of the bed-and-breakfast, he made more money than with his whole winemaking experience. He validates that to make money in the wine industry, you need a lot of money.

THE KENTUCKY BACK ROADS WINE TRAIL

The counties of Northern Kentucky have embraced their rich winemaking heritage. Today, there are several commercial wineries that span Bracken, Campbell and Kenton Counties. They've banded together and market themselves as the Back Roads Wine Trail. Driving through the picturesque rural Kentucky roads, one sees tobacco barns, stone walls, stone houses and remnants of a once rich winemaking past.

The focus of these wineries seems to be more on growing European hybrid grapes than native varietals, but at least two have experimented with the native Norton grape: Stonebrook Winery and Atwood Hill Winery. Many are on multigenerational historic farms, and one—Baker Bird in Augusta—is the most historic, having a legacy that goes back to before the Civil War.

Camp Springs is a hidden gem in the hills of Campbell County. Founded in the 1840s by German and Swiss immigrants from wine country, its hills are nestled with German vernacular fieldstone houses built before the Civil War and unique to our area and the United States. Most of the residents there today are fourth-generation and later descendants of the original founders. These Rhinelander Germanic immigrants grew grapes on the hillside, making their own wine and potentially supplying the Cincinnati wine houses like Longworth's.

One of the immigrant winemakers of Camp Springs was Andrew Ritter (1849–1916). He was born in Eschen, Liechtenstein, on the west side of the lower Rhine winemaking region. It was just south of the Swiss canton of St. Gallen, where many other northern Kentucky Catholics came from. His farm, which is still standing, contains a bank stone vaulted wine cellar and press room. The Ritters were part of the German Catholic community of St. Joseph in Camp Springs.

The Andrew Ritter farm complex in Camp Springs, Kentucky, including an 1880s wine house and vineyard. *Courtesy of Mark Ramler.*

Fast-forward 150 years, and now winemaking is coming back to the region. Four families are bringing back the centuries-old heritage of winemaking to the hills around Camp Springs on historic farms. These wineries are Camp Springs Vineyard, Stonebrook, Seven Wells and 12 Mile.

CAMP SPRINGS VINEYARD

The Camp Springs Vineyard on Four Mile Road was established in 2005 by co-owners and brothers Kevin and Chris Enzweiler. That year, they planted 200 Vidal Blanc grapes. The next year, they planted a second vineyard with 650 more Vidal Blanc vines. The brothers are descendants of Michael Enzweiler, who immigrated from Germany to Camp Springs in 1843. Their first harvest came in 2007, and then in 2008, a third field was planted with 900 Cabernet Franc vines. At this point, the hillside winery and tasting room were built, and they reaped a harvest of two thousand pounds of Vidal Blanc. With their vines continually maturing, they reaped a harvest of more than seven thousand pounds of Vidal Blanc grapes the next season, and their tasting room opened in October 2009 at the Camp Springs Herbst Tour. Adding to their variety of grapes, in 2011, fifty Steuben vines were added, and another red variety, the St. Croix, was planted in 2015, which gave its first harvest in the fall of 2019 for winemaking. With the addition of a kitchen, they can host weddings, rehearsal dinners, birthdays and other celebratory events at the picturesque winery.

Stonebrook Winery

Stonebrook Winery is a small farm/family winery in Camp Springs, Kentucky, converted from a tobacco and livestock farm. Operated by the Dennis Walter family, it is dedicated to crafting high-quality grape and fruit wines. The family have been tending the vineyards since 2000 and making wine since 2005. Visitors can taste their wines on site in their renovated 1890 farmhouse with magnificent hillside vineyard views. Varieties grown are Vidal Blanc and Cayuga White. A smaller quantity of Cynthiana Norton and Vignoier, Cabernet Franc, Marechal Foch and Concord are also grown.

Seven Wells

Seven Wells Vineyard & Winery began in 2004 when four hundred grapevines were planted on the Greg Wehrman family farm in Grants Lick, Kentucky. More vines were planted, and the vineyard grew to five acres. Grape varieties have included Chardonnay, Cabernet Franc, Traminette, Dornfelder, Noiret and Kentucky standards Chambourcin and Vidal Blanc, as well as a short-lived dalliance with Merlot. Seven Wells crafts a variety of wines to suit a variety of tastes, from full-bodied dry reds to sweet whites.

12 Mile Creek Winery

12 Mile Creek Winery is a small farm and family owned and operated winery established in 2016. It is set in the foothills of southern Campbell County, overlooking 12 Mile Creek on Route 10. Tami and Kevin Stewart opened the doors for tastings in July 2017. They produce award-winning wines by combining new ideas with old family recipes from Kevin's dad, John, who made homemade wine for his family. They produce fruit wines like blackberry and a unique jalapeño wine. Other varieties include Chambourcin, Catawba, Concord, Cabernet Franc, Diamond, Edelweiss and Corot Noir.

ATWOOD HILL WINERY AND VINEYARD

The Atwood Hill Winery and Vineyard sits on the sixth-generation Clinkenbeard family farm, established in 1918 in Kenton County, Kentucky. The original farmhouse, named the Farmstead, which houses the tasting room, can be booked for private events. The three-acre vineyards were planted in 2005 and 2006 with French hybrid varietals Vidal Blanc, Cayuga White and Chambourcin Red. A small number of Norton was planted in 2011, and a wine was made in 2017. However, the owners decided that the Norton was not productive enough for their goals and pulled up the vines in 2018, even though their Norton made a fantastic wine.

All the grapes are hand picked, and the destemming, crushing and pressing are all done on site. The wine is aged from nine months to two years in stainless steel tanks before bottling. Oak barrels are also used to enhance the taste. Atwood showcases fourteen different types of wine, all of which can be enjoyed on site.

BAKER BIRD WINERY

Baker Bird Winery in Augusta, Kentucky, is the oldest standing commercial winery in the country, and it has the distinction of being the only winery to survive a Civil War battle. Early in the city's history, Augusta was a popular shipping port. Products shipped from Augusta included tobacco, hemp, livestock and wine. Bracken County, Kentucky, reached its height of wine production in the 1870s, producing about thirty thousand gallons of wine annually. During the mid-1800s, European immigrants helped establish a thriving wine industry in Augusta. The Ulerick, Sliefnatin, Switzer, Heine and Dlifiner families brought their winemaking knowledge to the area in the 1850s. At the center of the enterprise was Abraham Baker Jr., who built what is today Baker Bird Winery in the 1850s.

When the Civil War came to Augusta in September 1862, Baker's wine cellar was used as a place of refuge by many citizens. John Hunt Morgan's forces, led by General Basil Duke, entered Augusta from the south. The Confederate troops met resistance from the home guard, led by Joshua Bradford. Bradford was an ovarian surgeon and a large winegrower in Augusta. Three years after the battle, Bradford sold ten thousand gallons of native wine from his vineyard at $2.50 per gallon to the Longworth Wine House.

The winery and wine cellars of the Baker Bird Winery in Augusta, Kentucky. *Courtesy of the author.*

Today, Baker Bird doesn't grow its own grapes, but rather produces a variety of Vidal Blanc whites and a variety of reds made from Chambourcin and Cabernet Franc. The original forty-foot-by-ninety-foot wine cellar built into the hill makes an excellent place for an event.

CINCINNATI WINE TODAY

Ohio today is a top ten producing wine state, fermenting 1.1 million gallons of the juice annually. We have 340 wineries throughout the state and 1.37 million wine tourists cavorting around them annually. Today's viticulture technologies allow most of the wineries to use hybrid *Vitus vinifera* or European grapes, but some are still preserving our winemaking past by using Catawba and other native *Vitus labrusca* and *Vitus aestivalis* American grapes. University research has made available many new and exciting hybrids and crossbreeds. While the vineyards that decorated our river hills are a memory, Cincinnati's influence in the wine world is still prominent.

Meier's Winery is a Cincinnati gem as the city's oldest continually operating winery and second oldest in Ohio. Its roots go all the way back to the Catawba Craze of the 1850s, and its Lake Erie and New Richmond, Ohio vineyards preserved the native grapes of Catawba, Delaware, Norton and Ives, all of which were grown during the height of our Cincinnati wine industry. There are several other wineries of note that continue to use the Catawba grape in their wines. Vinoklet Winery in Colerain Township and Meranda-Nixon Winery in Clermont County near New Richmond are the last two estate wineries left. Both grow and make wine of their own Catawba grapes, and Meranda-Nixon is the last local to grow its own Norton grapes for wine. Henke Winery carries on the wonderful wine legacy of Westwood and makes its own Norton from Ohio-grown grapes grown near New Richmond. Skeleton Root, in Cincinnati's old Germanic enclave of Over-the-Rhine, is the newest kid on the block, making Catawba still and sparkling wines with a respect for the methods of Longworth. It also makes a 60 percent Norton/40 percent Syrah blend made with Missouri Nortons. And although not a Cincinnati winery, Heineman Winery in Put-in-Bay, Ohio, deserves to be celebrated. It is a four-generation family-owned winery, the oldest continually operating in Ohio, and like Meier, it operated through Prohibition. It also deserves respect as the caretaker of Ohio's legacy Isle St. George vineyards and for preserving the Ives grape cultivated first in Cincinnati.

Sadly, no Catawba brandy or Catawba bitters are being made locally. This leaves an opportunity for a passionate new entrepreneur. Remember, Catawba brandy, while delicious, also cures summer complaints, seasonal dysentery, diarrhea and the gout. And President Lincoln used locally made Catawba brandy as a medicinal supplement. Who could produce a better testimonial?

JOHANN MICHAEL MEIER AND HIS VINEYARD

Meier's Wine Cellars is Cincinnati's oldest continually operating winery (1890) and Ohio's second oldest after Heinemann's (1888) in Put-in-Bay, Ohio. It is Ohio's largest winery, with a tank capacity nearing 2 million gallons of wine. It sits nestled in the Cincinnati neighborhood of Silverton, where it has been since 1906, when Johann Michael Meier bought the six-acre plot next to the railroad for good logistics. Today, it is owned by Paul Lux, the nephew of the owner of Luxco, from which he bought it in 2017. Meier's no longer owns its own vineyards and sources its grapes from a variety of growers. It still makes its classic still and Sparkling Catawba wines, sherries and non-alcoholic grape juice.

The founder, Johann Michael Meier (1830–1926), immigrated to America in 1854 from Baden-Wuertemburg. His accommodations in steerage were far from deluxe, but the bonus was that he met a pretty girl from his homeland, Kunigunda Siedenfaden, whom he married when they landed. Johann had several friends from Baden-Wuertemburg who had already settled in Reading, Ohio, a small town north of Cincinnati. He and his wife joined the community of St. John Lutheran Church.

His friends offered him odd jobs like table waiting, drink-slinging at taverns and manual labor gigs that put sausage on the table. But being an entrepreneur, he wanted his own land and wanted to be his own boss.

Left: Johann Michael Meier, an immigrant from Baden-Wuertemburg, started growing grapes in a vineyard that is now the site of Kenwood Mall. *Courtesy of Meier's Winery.*

Below: An image of the original Meier farm and vineyard on what is now the site of Kenwood Mall. *Courtesy of Meier's Winery.*

Through the help of the clergy at St. John's, he was able to make an application for his homestead of 164 acres on the Cincinnati-Zanesville Pike at what is now the Kenwood Plaza Shopping Center.

On his new land, he was able to establish himself as a grain and livestock farmer. But Johann also wanted to plant a small vineyard—he could have a glass of wine with dinner, as he did in the fatherland. So, he sent back home for native grapevines of the *Vitus vinifera* family from Germany and planted his first American vineyard. But what he found, like many immigrants before, was that these European vines couldn't stand the harsh winters and the mildew caused by high humidity and early summers of the area. By this

Left: Johann Conrad Meier, J. Michael Meier's son, discovered how to make unfermented Catawba wine juice. *Courtesy of Meier's Winery.*

Below: The Meiers bought the current Silverton site in 1906. *Courtesy of Meier's Winery.*

MEIER'S WINE CELLARS

time, his son, John Conrad Meier, was helping out with chores of the farm, with a special interest in the vineyard. Johann had heard of Longworth's success with the Catawba grape and converted the vineyards.

Cincinnatians traveled to the Meier farm in the country to fill their casks with Catawba wine. In 1895, another opportunity opened for John Conrad Meier and his family. That year, John Conrad went to take a sample of his Catawba wine one night from the wine cellar on the Kenwood farm. He siphoned it out into a demijohn, which he placed in the kitchen. While he was cleaning up for supper, his younger sister, Anna, poured a glass for herself of this young wine. What she thought would be dry white Catawba wine was actually unfermented sweet Catawba grape juice. Something had prevented it from starting its second fermentation. John Conrad figured out the process for making stable non-alcoholic grape juice from this moment and incorporated as the J.C. Meier Juice Company in 1905.

In 1922, John Conrad Meier passed away, and his daughter Helen's brother-in-law, Henry O. Sonneman, took over the ownership and operation of Meier's. He was a sommelier of some renown and had traveled in Europe, becoming fond of Spanish sherry. So, he brought back the Spanish numbering system of Europe and began making Meier sherry. The lower the sherry number, the drier it is; the higher the number, the sweeter. A sherry is aged four to seven years in small casks and then transferred to larger casks for more aging. Then it is bottled and bin aged. Sonneman's favorite sherry was a long-aged, rich-bodied, fragrant one called Oloroso. He liked a particular Oloroso fortified for body and depth. Concerned with the supply of his favorite sherry during World War II, Sonneman developed the solera process to make the first Meier's #44 Cream Sherry, which came to the market in the 1950s.

The Cream Sherry was a favorite of Senator John F. Kennedy, and it was also supplied for the Governor's Ball during the presidency of Jimmy Carter. Famous singer and ventriloquist performer Rudy Vallée loved Meier's wines, particularly the Mellow Burgundy and the Sparkling Burgundy, and recommended them to friends and fans in the 1950s and 1960s.

The sparkling grape juice is what saved Meier's through Prohibition, when so many other wineries closed shop. Meier's made altar wine for churches and also sold yeast packets. What the customer did when he got home was his own business. It was during this time that the famous giant Juice Jug was built in the front of the winery property to dispense glasses of juice for five cents.

In 1938, the company reincorporated as Meier's Wine Cellars, and the bar, restaurant and outdoor wine garden were built in 1940. Under Sonneman's leadership, Meier's bought a 350-acre vineyard on North Bass Island or Isle St. George in Lake Erie that supplied the majority of its grapes for production. It is the only island wine appellation in North America. The island is an area of about one square mile located in western Lake Erie in Ottawa County, Ohio. It is the smallest and northernmost of the three Bass islands, only 1.25 miles from Canada.

Henry passed away in 1974, and in 1976, Meier's sold out of the family to Paramount Distilleries in Cleveland, Ohio. It closed the restaurant and garden and streamlined the operation into a tasting room and retail store.

The giant Catawba juice bottle from which was sold non-alcoholic grape juice for five cents per glass. *Courtesy of Meier Winery.*

Robert Gottesman (born in 1918), the owner of Paramount, had a vision for better wines in Ohio and propelled a major revival in the lagging Ohio wine industry. In 1979, he bought the Mantey Winery in Venice, Ohio, which became the Sandusky winery of Meier's. He pioneered the planting of *Vitus vinifera*, or European grapes, in the Meier's vineyard in Isle St. George, and it became the largest *Vitus vinifera* varietal vineyard in Ohio. As an avid fisherman, Gottesman also developed a white wine that he thought would pair well with Lake Erie's native walleye, and so was born Meier's Walleye White, a blend of 90 percent Riesling and 10 percent Gewurztraminer.

Meier's also owned the 180-acre JacJan Vineyards in the Clermont Valley near New Richmond, Ohio, where it grew the Ives grape. It also planted Catawba and French hybrid vines. The vineyard had a grafting area and a special greenhouse for propagating grafted vines. A failure of the Ives vineyard in the mid-1970s prompted Meier's to sell it to a real estate developer, who leased the vineyards for a short time to Morrow Ohio's Valley Vineyards.

In September 2011, Luxco Inc., based out of St. Louis, purchased Meier's winery. Luxco makes the liquor brands Pearl Vodka and Everclear. Six years later, in October 2018, Luxco sold to the owners' nephew, Paul Lux. Paul has continued to expand the business by continuing to make wine but also co-packing for other companies' liquor products, with the large tank capacity it has on site.

Meier's mission remains to produce high-quality wines from Native American *Vitus labrusca* grape varietals like the Catawba. Its current wine list features more than thirty wines, including classic sweet, table, dessert and fruit wines under the Meier's label, as well as Reiem Sparkling Wines. It also produces eight flavors of sparkling non-alcoholic beverages under the John C. Meier Juice Company Label. One more unique brand of wine it makes is the Ohio Haute Sauterne, a sweet wine made with Delaware, Catawba and Niagara grapes. The future looks bright and sparkling for Meier's to continue on for many more decades as Cincinnati's legacy winery.

Henke Winery: Carrying on the Westwood Wine Legacy

I found Henke Winery in college, when it was located in the old Drivikas Greek candy store and soda fountain in Winton Place, now called Spring Grove Village. I fell in love with its seafood pizza and its wine. At the time in 1996, it was one of the two urban wineries in Cincinnati, and it was a rare pleasure to have Cincinnati-made wine.

Then, in 2001, Joe Henke bought a larger space in the historic Cincinnati winemaking area of Westwood—in the former Window Garden restaurant, next to the former Habig restaurant, famous for its Concord Grape Pie. But the history connection was coincidence. Joe was looking for more cellar space for his rapidly expanding winery. He was tired of bumping his head and straining his back carrying his vintage German bottle capping machine into the short basement in Winton Place.

Joe is a true winemaker but started as a hobbyist. If you're looking for Longworth eccentricity, you might find it in his ponytail, but unlike Longworth, he is methodical and hands-on in his winemaking. In 1973, his sister and brother-in-law were living in Erie, Pennsylvania, which is Concord grape country. They thought that winemaking would be something Joe would enjoy doing. So, he made a Granache Rosé, and it turned out pretty good. He moved on to other wines and started taking them around to other wineries. The other wineries thought that Joe's wines were pretty good. In the 1970s, most Ohio wineries were making sweet wines, and quality control was not very good. Bad fermentations caused problems with acetone generation. Most wineries were just adding yeast and sugar to their pressed juice and letting it go on its own, without any testing. Roland Reason pushed the Ohio wine industry into testing and creating higher-quality wines with his program.

Joe solicited winemaking advice from Ohio sages like Dr. Konstantin Frank, who planted the first *vinifera* grapes in Ohio; Arnie Esterer of Markko Vineyards in Northwest Ohio; and Todd Steiner, head of the enology program at Ohio State University. Joe had some barrels made and started getting serious about wines. He opened the winery in 1996 in Winton Place.

In 2021, Joe celebrated his twenty-fifth wine-aversary in the anonymity of the COVID-19 pandemic. Every year, to celebrate its anniversary, Henke hosts a cork sculpture contest that has seen some amazing creations, including a working clock, a pirate ship (with Henke label sails) and a variety of other creative forms. Maybe after the pandemic is well and truly over, someone will make a COVID virus particle sculpture out of corks.

Left: Joe Henke stands proudly in front of a barrel of wine in his cellars in Westwood. *Courtesy of Joe Henke.*

Right: Joe Henke moved his winery from Winton Place to the former Window Garden Restaurant in Westwood in 2001. *Courtesy of the author.*

In 2013, Joe made his first Norton wine. Andrew Manning and his wife, Linda, wanted to start a vineyard with Nortons, and Joe helped them get the Ohio grant, which became St. Clair Vineyards in Winchester, Ohio. The Polar Vortex of 2014–15 put a huge wrench in the Norton crop. Joe is selling their 2016 Norton, which won a bronze medal at the United States' largest Norton wine competition and the Jefferson Cup in Missouri. Joe's 2017 and 2018 are still being aged in the cellar, but his 2018 won a silver at the Jefferson Cup. It's the most jammy of the three Nortons and the least acidic. But all three Nortons are spectacularly drinkable. He aspires to win the Jefferson Cup. 2020's local crops of Nortons are less prolific because of the early frost we had.

Joe makes about twenty-seven varieties of other wines in addition to his phenomenal Nortons to the tune of about four thousand gallons per year. He started making sparkling wine in 1998, and he's been making it ever since. He uses a unique process called "sur-lie" to make his Seyval and Chardonnay sparkling wines. It uses the lees, or the dead yeast cells killed by fermentation enzymes, to add beneficial textures and flavors of toast, cheese, buttermilk, floral elderflower and sweet nuttiness.

He has filled every nook and cranny in his wine cellar with tanks and barrels. The bottling area, which employs fifteen volunteers at bottling time, has a desk with shelves of hydrometers, testing devices and the obligatory bottle of Tums that comes with the territory of any hardworking man over the age of forty. He also has a cold storage facility in the back to age the blush wines. Add to that a one-ton press and destemming machine and Joe is set for bringing fabulous wines to Cincinnati for decades to come.

Vinoklet Winery: Born in the Soil of Colerain, with the Soul of Cincinnati

In the art of getting to know someone, there is usually an aspect that is so innate about them they just forget to tell you. For the big mustachioed Croatian Kreso Mikulic, who owns Vinoklet Winery in Colerain Township, that aspect is winemaker. For the last forty years, though, this is what everyone has known him to be. But before working as a winemaker, he was a carpenter, an aerospace engineer, an alpine skier and an Olympic gymnast—I would add grape guru and comedian to that list. He's like so many of the other Cincinnati wine barons, who led massively full Renaissance lifestyles. But winemaking was in his blood, and it called out to him.

Kreso brings generations of old-world muscle memory to American winemaking, but it's not from the Germanic Rhine region, which was home to our area's first vineyardists. Kreso's is a Mediterranean one. He grew up working his father's vineyard in Croatia, in a small village near the town of Split. Here, if you didn't make wine, people thought you were weird. From the age of five, he was crushing grapes for his father's wine. Some of his family members still own a winery in the Postup peninsular region, almost halfway between Split and Dubrovnik.

His mother bore thirteen kids, saying that God gave her this many to help work the vineyards. It was his mother who instilled his devotion to the Virgin Mary, in whose honor he has a water fountain grotto next to the outdoor pavilion at the winery. He brought back wine and rosaries for his customers from Medjagoria, where there is a sighting of the Virgin Mary substantiated as a miracle by the Catholic Church.

What do you need to become a wealthy winemaker? Lots of money, said Kreso. He talks about local winemakers who saw it as a business first instead of a heartfelt passion. That's a repeating story of our early winemakers. And for Kreso, having winemaking in his blood, he knows that it's a work of passion. He knows that one must love vines to be successful. He says that the best fertilizer for vines is your own shadow. Vines are selfish, he notes—they love to be visited and cared for. And they're temperamental. You may have a good crop one year and not a good one for several years. It takes a lot of work and patience with vines.

Croatian native Kreso Mikulic, the owner of Vinoklet Winery in Colerain Township. *Courtesy of Vinoklet Winery.*

He bought the thirty acres of Vinoklet in 1980 when it was just ravines and forest. He cleared the area, leveled off the ravines into rolling hills with seventeen thousand truckloads of dirt and planted his first vines, the native Catawba, in 1986, to make wines for friends. The vines died. He planted again; they died too. Then he planted a third time, one thousand vines; they took off and sprouted, and the rest is history.

He has the only commercial vineyard in Hamilton County. And if you come during the summer or fall seasons, you can see the groups of workers tending the vines.

In addition to native *labrusca* vines of Catawba and Niagara, Kreso grows European hybrids like the Traminer, Cabernet Sauvignon, Cab Franc, Chambourcin and Vidal Blanc. He says that the American grapes like Catawba, Concord and Niagara are too acidic and make better grape juice than wine. Kreso also admits that Cincinnati is really not a wine growing region because its summers are too humid and winters too harsh. The Catawba, for example, is only good to negative twenty-five degrees Fahrenheit. He makes more than twenty thousand gallons of wine per year and supplies about one hundred stores in the Cincinnati area, including Kroger, Meier, Jungle Jim and numerous smaller wine shops.

In 2020, he planted some new cold-hardy grapes developed by University of Minnesota called Petit Pearl, cultivated by Tom Plocher, a Minnesota grape breeder. He also has Frontenac and Etasa, both developed by University of Minnesota.

He talks about the experience customers get when they come to Vinoklet. They experience the sound of the rustling water of the paddle

A view of the Vinoklet vineyards and press house from the winery. *Courtesy of Vinoklet Winery.*

wheel and grotto fountain and the smell of smoked meat from the kitchen. They enjoy the sight of the beautiful west-facing sunset and the rolling hills of the ten acres of vineyard. While peace and serenity abound at Vinoklet, Kreso's early life was anything but. Growing up in the communist regime under Josip Tito was not all that peaceful, but he made do. He apprenticed as a carpenter and then got a degree in electrical engineering from the University of Zagreb. He proudly displays his vintage woodworking tools in the basement room and some of the electrical devices he made and patented during his career at GE.

Vinoklet is just what you want in a winery experience: a great meal in a great atmosphere overlooking the rolling hills of vineyards that house the grapes that made your wine. While the majority of his wines are estate wines made from the grapes on site, he still does buy grapes for wine in his top-of-the-line wine house. It has one two-and-a-half-ton press and a modern automated bottling line that can bottle three thousand per hour.

Kreso can seat five hundred people total in his several rooms in the complex, which he built himself. There's the main tasting room, with two wine-themed murals by Cincinnati artist Tracy Bezesky—much in the tradition of Nicholas Longworth's patronage of artists. The loft above houses all the instrumentation he used in his aerospace engineering years, designing engines for the B-1 bomber and Black Hawk helicopter. There's a private space seating sixty for weddings, a basement speakeasy with round booths and a dancefloor, an upstairs solarium, an outdoor pavilion and even the world's largest wine barrel, which can host private tastings and romantic dinners. This is truly an unrivaled Cincinnati experience. The west-facing hills frame some of the prettiest sunsets in Hamilton County—guests can see all the way to Indiana.

Kreso humbly says that his wine is drinkable, but his wines have won many awards. His brother Joe won the double-gold for Best Wine in the State of Ohio in 2015. The Tears of Joy Dry White won the gold medal for best wine at the 2018 Cincinnati International Wine Festival. The Cincinnati Dry Red—made of Merlot and Chambourcin grapes—has received several medals, like the silver and the double-gold at the Indy International Wine Competition. His Sunset Blush Semi-Sweet—made of native Catawba, Niagara and Vidal Blanc grapes—has won a silver at the Best of the Midwest Competition in 2018. The Vinoklet estate winery experience is a unique and enjoyable one not to be missed.

Meranda-Nixon Winery: Nailing the Norton in President Grant Country

One local winery that makes a great day trip is Meranda-Nixon Winery in Ripley, Ohio. Here you can live its mission—to sip, relax and repeat—while also taking in some phenomenal local historical sites. I visited Seth and Maura Meranda on a Saturday in July for a progressive tasting of their four years of Norton grape wines. They are an estate winery and one of the few in Ohio that grows the Norton. The great thing about an estate winery is that what you see is what you get. You can walk through the vineyards and see the grapes made into the wine you're sipping. They're all family run and operated, with the help of their four children and even some of their classmates.

Upon arriving, the first thing you see is their oldest Catawba vineyard as you pull into their tasting room and restaurant on Laycock Road. It's under an hour drive from downtown Cincinnati along Route 32 to 68; this allows you to stop at several of the farmers' markets along the way. You can

The Meranda family standing in front of the vineyard. *Courtesy of Maura Meranda.*

also take Route 52 along the scenic Ohio River, which will take you past some of the wine mansions and cellars from Clermont and Brown Counties' moment in our local wine industry, when vineyards lined the Ohio River hills from Coney Island to Ripley.

The Norton is a special grape. It was one of the native varieties in the 1860s proven to be more resistant to black rot, mildew and phylloxera than our beloved Catawba. It makes one of the most unique and deeply flavored red wines to this day—giving dark fruits like blackberry, plum, black cherry, cranberry, with subtle spiciness and other notes like tobacco, leather and coffee. Unlike the Catawba and Concord—which are now largely grown more north in the regions of the Lake Erie Islands, lakefront Pennsylvania and upper New York—the Norton today is primarily grown down here in the Ohio River Valley, the Piedmonts of Virginia and near St. Louis, Missouri.

Seth, who graduated from Ohio State's College of Agriculture, says that the Norton takes longer to establish—five to seven years versus the three to four years of most varietals of either native *labrusca* or European *viniferas*. He began planting his now twelve-plus acres of vineyards in 2006 on his grandfather's historic tobacco farm. But once the Norton is established, it requires little maintenance and makes a fabulously unique wine. Norton grapes, which have a smaller bunch than Catawbas and other varietals, are planted in north–south rows and leaf-pruned on the east side, which is a milder sun than the evening west side. Nortons, for their berry size, have a lot of seeds, and if picked too early, the seeds will impart a bell pepper flavor to the wine.

One modern vineyard problem is the Japanese beetle, a recent pest that oddly love eating Norton leaves, but Seth can solve that problem. The Norton is also sensitive to herbicide drift from GMO farmers who spray the neighboring corn or soybeans. Seth's three hunting dogs—who greeted me when I pulled into the vineyard—guard against raccoons, 'possums and deer eating the ripe grapes. And laser technology, which replaced neighbor-unfriendly carbon dioxide cannons, keeps away the birds.

Seth and I walked the vineyards as Maura let the Nortons breathe for my tasting. He showed the high cordon position of the Norton and the Catawba grapes and the lower VSP (vine shoot position) orientation of the European varietals they grow, such as Traminette, Chardonnay, Cab Franc and Cab Sauvignon. He works with his alma mater, Ohio State, and keeps up with Cornell research on experimental grapes; he said that the once popular Traminette grape is being replaced by a new diva, the Pinotage, a South African native.

A local history teacher came into the winery to enjoy a frozé, or frozen rosé, on the patio while Seth and I were talking wine history, and she added to the discussion. She lived not far away on her husband's family's farm, which three generations ago was also a winery, growing native grapes. Maura said that the frozé and their wine slushies are the gateway for younger non-wine-drinkers. Their evening dinners, which integrate veggies grown on their farm, are a great way to enjoy their wines and take in the vineyard lifestyle.

Maura said that Europeans who visit always go away with their Norton wines because they're a unique American wine that is unlike any European red. The 2014 Norton to me has a blackberry- and cranberry-forward flavor, with slight elements of leather and a citrusy, lemongrass finish. The 2015 Norton is full-bodied with dark fruit and oak flavors. I tasted a jammier flavor with a more tart finish than the 2014. The 2016 to me was more oak-forward than any of the others. They describe it as deep red with raspberry aromas and hints of coffee and bittersweet chocolate. The 2017—for which they won a gold medal at the Mid-America Wine Competition—has a plum flavor to me, while they describe it as a spicy black cherry. I even got to taste their unreleased 2019 Norton, which has the same dark fruit flavor but is smooth and light. I love them all for different reasons—they all have subtle but noticeable flavor differences. Seth said that the 2020 Norton crop is not as prolific as years past because of our droughty summer, so I look forward to seeing what unique wine it makes.

They make a wonderful estate Sparkling Catawba that is better than any prosecco I have tasted. It's not as sweet as a prosecco, nor as dry as most brut sparkling wines, which makes it a refreshing summer sparkling wine. The Sparkling Catawba makes an amazing breakfast mimosa to go with your crab eggs Benedict or goetta sandwich.

The Merandas have sold their grapes and juice to neighboring Valley Vineyards and the Verona Vineyards Winery near Rabbit Hash, Kentucky. But Meranda-Nixon is one of the only estate Nortons made in Ohio. The other is made in Vinton County, Ohio, past Portsmouth, Ohio, by La Petit Chevalier Vineyards.

The Norton was supposedly President Ulysses S. Grant's favorite red wine. He bought cases of it from Missouri vineyards to stock the White House cellars. And he grew up in the area of the Meranda-Nixon winery. The small cabin of his birthplace is on State Route 52 in nearby Point Pleasant. And his boyhood home is in Georgetown, only about fifteen minutes away. Making a trip to Meranda-Nixon can be made into an amazing and delicious one-day or overnight stay to take in the Ohio River and the historic sites in and around Ripley, Ohio.

Skeleton Root: An Urban Winery
Respecting the Longworth Legacy

It's no coincidence that Kate MacDonald chose an old building in Over-the-Rhine for her urban winery. It was here, in the coffee houses of this neighborhood of Germanic immigrants, where the majority of Catawba wine was consumed. And she is making Catawba still and sparkling wines in the methodology of Old Nick.

A graduate of Colerain High school, she trained as an engineer and first took a hook in winemaking while living in the Finger Lakes region of New York, where Longworth's former sparkling winemaker Jules Masson went after Longworth's death to proliferate American grape sparkling wines. She followed her interest to California, like Longworth's Missouri nemesis George Husmann, the master of the Norton grape. As she studied wine history, MacDonald was surprised that Longworth in her hometown had been an early father of the industry.

An ad for the Skelton Root Direct Press Wine Club shows its facility on McMicken Avenue in Over-the-Rhine. *Courtesy of Skeleton Root Winery.*

In 2016, she and her partner, Josh Jackson, returned to Cincinnati and opened Skeleton Root. The name is a nod to resurrecting fruit from a historic vine. She sources Catawbas from the Lake Erie region and her *vinifera* European hybrids like Sauvignon Blanc and Semillon from a Clarksville, Ohio vineyard in Clinton County near Wilmington, where she hopes to grow local Catawbas. She's also found a vineyard site in Indiana, the area of Swiss winemaker James Dufour, who taught Longworth about the Cape grape. She plans to grow Catawbas and other American *labrusca* varieties there.

With her background in engineering, MacDonald understands Catawba chemistry. Because of the shorter growing season, the Catawba, which has larger berries than European grapes, never fully develops its sugars, so it results in a lower-alcohol-content, acidic wine that needs to be aged a bit longer. She says that this is not a flaw, but rather a distinctive characteristic of our region's wines.

She makes a Sparkling Catawba that is delightfully refreshing, but her pride and joy is the still Catawba wine. She ages her still Catawba wine for four years in European oak to mellow the harsh malic acid into a smoother lactic acid. This still Catawba has been described as having notes of rhubarb and the crunchy greenness of cucumber. She intervenes as little as possible to let the unique flavor of the Catawba speak for itself. The hard-to-describe flavor of the Catawba, and of many American grapes, is described as "foxy," or having a wild muskiness. This is what has steered a lot of winemakers away from using Catawba, as well as sparking others to make sweeter wines from Catawba to mask the musk and acidity.

The winery is located in a nondescript early 1900s warehouse on McMicken Avenue, on the northern edge of the neighborhood. You sort of feel like you're walking into a speakeasy as you wind up the steep, narrow steps to the second-floor tasting wine bar. It's rustic chic, elegant and comfortable. Couches and comfy chairs surround an oversized 1850s lithograph of a romanticized Longworth vineyard on the Ohio River. You can nestle into one of the corners or at the long bar and get a well-curated tasting of any of the ten wines they have on tap by one of the knowledgeable bartenders. You can even take a walk next to the bar area and see the production and storage facilities on site. There's a private room that can seat one hundred and another smaller room, the Barn, that has wine aging in oak barrels lining the wall.

Skeleton Root is an excellent way to drink native by sipping on Cincinnati's Catawba legacy and pondering our winemaking past in the neighborhood where it was enjoyed.

REVEL WINERY

Revel is a boutique urban winery, full bar and wine collective that opened in April 2017. Located in an 1885 building in Over-the-Rhine, it specializes in small-batch wines made on site, like its Cabernet Sauvignon, a silver medalist at the 2020 Cincinnati International Wine Festival. Other handcrafted wines include its Malbec, Sangiovese, Carménère, Black Sheep Blanc, Black Sheep Rosé and Black Sheep Red Blend Rouge. Revel wines are juiced and destemmed for fermentation in Wilkymacky Alley behind the winery, with European hybrid grapes sourced from California, Washington and Chile using a process that originated in Italy by the Maieron family. Founders Anthony Maieron and John Coleman made wine together for thirteen years in Maieron's basement in a tradition derived from his Italian immigrant parents. Alex Sena, head vintner, spent years managing Chateau Pomijie vineyard and winery in Guilford, Indiana, before joining the Revel OTR team. He ages the wines in the basement, which holds up to sixty barrels of wine. Revel hopes to become an iconic neighborhood meeting area.

SELECTED BIBLIOGRAPHY

Interviews

Brandstetter, Bob. Phone interview with author, March 23, 2021.
Heinemann, Dustin, Heinemann Winery. Interview with author, 2020.
Henke, Joe, Henke Winery. Interview with author, August 18, 2020.
Meranda, Seth, and Maura Meranda, Meranda-Nixon Winery. Interview with author, July 18, 2020.
Mikulic, Kresco, Vinoklet Winery. Interview with author, August 7, 2020.
Moore, Stephanie, Meier Winery. Interview with author, June 24, 2020.
Schmidt, Mark, Monte Cassino Bed & Breakfast. Interview with author, July 2, 2020.

Letters

Amos, Lawrence. Letter to Giles Richards, March 29, 1855. From the Gilbert-Richards Collection at the Miami University Library.
Burnham, L.S. Letter to Giles Richards, October 13, 1860. From the Gilbert-Richards Collection at the Miami University Library.
Coombs, A.D. Letter to Giles Richards, March 7, 1850. From the Gilbert-Richards Collection at the Miami University Library.
Huber, Father Celestine. Letter to Father Aurelius Stehle, Archabbot of St. Vincent, February 21, 1919. From Archives of St. Vincent Abbey.

Longworth, Nicholas. Letter to Giles Richards. April 21, 1850. From the Gilbert-Richards Collection at the Miami University Library.

Otto, Father. Letter to Father Leander Schnerr, Archabbot of St. Vincent, October 9, 1894. Translated from German. From Archives of St. Vincent Abbey.

Richards, Giles. Letter to Christian Schniecke, October 17, 1860. From the Gilbert-Richards Collection at the Miami University Library.

Richards, Giles. Letter to Christian Schniecke, October 16, 1860. From the Gilbert-Richards Collection at the Miami University Library.

Richards, W. Letter to his father, Giles Richards, October 22, 1850. From the Gilbert-Richards Collection at the Miami University Library.

Wimmer, Father Luke. Letter to Father Boniface Wimmer, Archabbot of St. Vincent, 1884. Translated from German. From Archives of St. Vincent Abbey.

Magazines and Newspapers

American Horticultural Review: A Yearbook of Horticultural Progress for the Professional and Amateur Gardener. "Longworth School of Vines." 1867.

Breetzke, David. "'Toto, We're Not in Napa Valley Anymore': The Viticulture Industry on Prospect Hill." *Bulletin of the Kenton County Historical Society* (July/August 2014). Covington, Kentucky.

Champlin, Charles. "Vacation Memory: In Quiet French Valley, a Search for Things Past." *Los Angeles Times*, September 15, 1991.

Cincinnati Commercial. "Cincinnati Horticultural Society." September 3, 1866.

Cincinnati Commercial Gazette. "Longworth Wine House." June 8, 1869.

Cincinnati Commercial Tribune. "Famous Old Time House Will Be Sold by Law." May 5, 1904.

Cincinnati Enquirer. "American Wine-Growers Association." August 16, 1880.

———. "American Wine-Growers Association." February 12, 1872.

———. "Buckhorn. A Vine Clad Cottage in Which Wm. J. Flagg and His Wife Lived as Hermits for Five Years." December 25, 1894.

———. "Cincinnati Horticultural Association." December 28, 1868.

———. "Cincinnati Horticultural Association—Their Regular Meeting." January 4, 1869.

———. "Cincinnati Horticultural Society." January 25, 1869.

———. "Dater: Pioneer Pork Packer of This City Passed Away at His Home in Westwood." April 22, 1904.

———. "Daughter of One of Cincinnati's First Citizens Was Mrs. Oehler, Who Will Be Buried Today." 1917.

———. "Death of an Old Citizen of Lick Run." February 7, 1886.

———. "Exposition Commissioners." October 31, 1879.

———. "Facts and Fancies." October 8, 1901.

———. "Fruit Distillery: To Be Put in Operation on the Werk Estate." March 5, 1897.

———. "The Golden Era: A Family Reunion on Bogen Heights." January 22, 1885.

———. "Moves House to Expand Business." March 2, 1948.

———. "The Old Lower River Road in the Early Days of Cincinnati." September 13, 1903.

———. "Phillip Metz Dead: Was Proprietor of Famous Wine Garden in Lick Run." September 30, 1911.

———. "Reports of the Cincinnati Horticultural Society of the First Annual Fair." November 6, 1843.

———. "Tailors of Early Cincinnati." April 26, 1896

———. "Uncle Joe Celebrates His Eighty-Third Birthday." December 12, 1892.

———. "Uncle Joe Siefert: A Pioneer Resident Passes Away at a Ripe Old Age." August 8, 1894.

———. "When Eden Park Was the Vineyard of a Citizen." February 11, 1923.

———. "Wine-Growers: A Meeting of the American Association in Plainville." August 14, 1881.

———. "The Wine Growing Interest of Hamilton County." August 22, 1873.

Cincinnati Enquirer Sunday Magazine. "Smallest Church in This County" (August 27, 1922).

Cist, Charles. "Native Wine." *New York Times*, September 24, 1852.

Debow's Review 13 (1853).

Debow's Review 12, no. 2 (February 1852).

Deutscher Pioneer Verein von Cincinnati. "Biographieren der verstorbenen Mitglieder." June 30, 1905. Publisher Chas F. Loz, Cincinnati, Ohio.

Eastern Hills Journal. "I Wandered Through the Village: The Sesquicentennial Story of Madisonville: Chapter V." June 24, 1959.

Grayson, Frank Y. "Historic Spots in Greater Cincinnati." *Cincinnati Times Star*, November 14, 1932.

Hickey, James T. "The Lincoln Account at the Corneau & Diller Drug Store, 1849–1861, a Springfield Tradition." *Journal of the Illinois State Historical Society Lincolniana* 77, no. 1 (Spring 1984).

Marshall, Lindsay. "Sedamsville Sanitation: Urban Archeaology." *Heritage Ohio*, May 15, 2014.

Maryland Farmer 4, no. 7. "Longworth Wine House" (July 1867).

Miller, Mary McGregor. "The Warder Family: A Short History." Clark County Historical Society, Springfield, Ohio, 1957.

Prairie Farmer. "Cincinnati Grapes Letter from Nicholas Longworth to Editor" (October 1848).

Prairie Farmer 8, no. 12. "Strawberry Correction" (December 1848).

Prairie Farmer 9, no. 11. "The Vintage in Kentucky" (November 1849).

Rural Farmer 22 (1867): 313.

Schlachter, Roberta L. "Dr. John Aston Warder." *Queen City Heritage* 47, no. 2 (Summer 1989).

Scientific American 8, no. 48. "American Wine" (August 13, 1853): 379.

Walston, Mark. *Bethesda Magazine*. "The Great Grape: How Vines from a Clarksburg Garden Helped Establish America's Fledgling Wine Industry." December 10, 2018.

Western Horticultural Review 2. "The Cincinnati Horticultural Society" (October 1851–September 1852): 242.

Western Horticultural Review 2. "Mr. Barnum on Wine" (October 1851–September 1852): 30.

Western Horticultural Review 2. "Mr. Schumann's Reply to Mr. Barnum" (October 1851–September 1852): 90.

Western Horticultural Review 2. "Schumann on Sweet Wines" (October 1851–September 1852): 171.

Western Horticultural Review 1, no. 2. "The Frontispiece" (November 1850).

Other Resources

Daniel H. Horne Lease to Bernard Wintziger. Executors of the Longworth Estate, April 1, 1865.

Diamond Jubilee Booklet. St. Joseph Church, Covington, Kentucky, 1934, 11–13.

Flagg, Melzer. "Remarks on the Culture of the Grape and the Manufacture of Wine in the Western United States." Cincinnati Horticultural Society, Cincinnati, Ohio, 1846.

George Fein Lease to Albert Schmidt. Hamilton County Ohio Recorder's Office, Book 114, 573.

Harmeling, Sister Deborah, OSB. "The Story of Covington's Monte Cassino." Covington, KY, 1969.

History of St. Stephens Church: 100ᵗʰ Anniversary. Cincinnati, OH: St. Stephens Church, 1967.

Longworth's Wine House. No. 113 East Sixth Street. Sparkling and Still Native Wines, Catawba, Isabela, etc. Cincinnati, OH: W.P. and F.P. Anderson, 1866.

Madeira Historical Society. "Madeira A City in 1960." 50ᵗʰ Anniversary Edition. Cincinnati, Ohio.

Monte Cassino. Annual cash statements, 1888–1925. Archives of St. Vincent Archabbey.

Ramey, Bern C. "The Story of Meier's 44 Cream Sherry." Meier's Wine Cellars.

Rentz, Rosemary, Sebastian Rentz family. Handwritten notes, 1988. Delhi Historical Society Collection.

Schenot, Elaine. Information on the Jergens family of Dayton, Ohio, 2019. rootsweb.com.

Schumann, Arthur M. *History and Genealogy of Charles Schumann (1795–1858).* West Milton, OH: Bowtie Publishing Company, 1995.

Valentin Muller Lease to Albert Schmidt. Hamilton County Ohio Recorder's Office, Book 125, 633.

Wirtner, Father Modestus, OSB. Report to St. Vincent Archabbey, September 1917.

Books

Buchanan, Robert. *A Treatise on the Cultivation of the Grape.* Cincinnati, OH: Wright Ferris & Company Printers, 1850.

Burke, Marie Welch. *Down by the Old Mill Race: The Early History of Plainville and the Wooster Pike Area from the Beginning to Terrace Park, Ohio, 1794–1971.* Cincinnati, OH: self-published, 1973.

Butler, James L. *Indiana Wine: A History.* Bloomington: Indiana University Press, 2001.

Cangi, Ellen Corwin. *From Viticulture to American Culture: The History of the Ohio River Valley Meyers Estate, 1845–1965.* Cincinnati, OH: Young & Klein Inc., 1983.

Chambrun, Clara Longworth. *Making of Nicholas Longworth: Annals of an American Family.* N.p.: Ray Long & Richard R. Smith, 1937.

Champlin, Charles. *Back There Where the Past Was: A Small-Town Boyhood.* Syracuse, NY: Syracuse University Press, 1999.

Duba, Larry, and Sue Schuler Brunsman. *The History of Delhi Township.* Cincinnati, OH: Delhi Township American Revolution Bicentennial Commission, 1976.

Flagg, William J. *Three Seasons in European Vineyards*. New York: Harper Brothers, 1869.

Ford, Henry A., and Kate B. Ford. *History of Hamilton County with Illustrations and Biographical Sketches*. Cincinnati, OH: L.A. Williams and Company, 1881.

Gerstacker, Friedrich. *Neue Reisen durch die Veriengten Staaten, Mexiko, Ecuador, Westindien, und Venezuela*. Vol. 1. Jena, DE: Hermann Costenobl, 1868–69, 85–103.

Greve, Charles Theodore. *Centennial History of Cincinnati and Representative Citizens*. Cincinnati, OH: Biographical Publishing Company, 1904.

Hudson, Cattel, and McKee Linda Jones. *Pennsylvania Wine: A History*. Charleston, SC: The History Press, 2012.

Husmann, George. *Cultivation of the Native Grape, and Manufacture of American Wines*. New York: George E. and F.W. Woodward, 1866.

Kenny, Daniel J. *Illustrated Cincinnati*. Cincinnati, OH: George E. Stevens & Company, 1879.

Kliman, Todd. *The Wild Vine: A Forgotten Grape and the Untold Story of American Wine*. New York: Crown Publishing Group, 2010.

Mackay, Charles. *Life and Liberty in America: Sketches of a Tour in the United States and Canada in 1857–1858*. N.p.: Cosimo Classics Travel & Exploration, n.d.

McConville, G. Terrence, and Fred L. Rutherford. *Pioneers of the Lower Little Miami Valley*. Cincinnati, OH: Mariemont Preservation Foundation, 2005.

Mersch, Christine. *Delhi: Cincinnati's Westside*. Charleston, SC: Arcadia Publishing, 2005.

Mosler, Max. *Historic Brighton*. Cincinnati, OH, 1902.

Potter, Eliza. *A Hairdresser's Experience in High Life*. Cincinnati, OH, 1859.

Reemelin, Charles. *Life of Charles Reemelin, in German: From 1814–1892, Written by Himself, in Cincinnati, Between 1890 and 1892*. Cincinnati, OH, n.d.

———. *The Vine Dresser's Manual, Illustrated Treatise: Vineyards and Winemaking*. New York: C.M. Saxton & Company, 1856.

Schumann, Charles. *The Culture of the Grape, Thoroughly Explained*. Cincinnati, OH: Robinson & Jones, 1845.

Shields, David S. *Pioneering American Wine: Writings of Nicholas Herbemont Master Viticulturist*. Atlanta: University of Georgia Press, 2009.

Stevens, Linda Walker. *What Wonderous Life: The World of George Husmann*. Hermann, MO: Hermann University Press, 2002.

Taft, Eleanor Gholson. *Hither and Yon on Indian Hill*. Cincinnati, OH: Indian Hill Garden Club, 1969.

Twain, Mark. *Mark Twain's Own Autobiography: The Complete and Authoritative Edition*. Vol. 1. Berkeley: University of California Press, 2010.

Williams, Byron. *History of Clermont and Brown Counties Ohio: From the Earliest Historical Times Down to the Present*. Milford, OH: Hobart Publishing, 1913.

ABOUT THE AUTHOR

Dann Woellert has been writing and speaking about regional food and drink for a decade. He's traveled the region, walking the vineyards and sipping native wine with the mission to bring the Ives and Norton grapes back to Cincinnati. He thinks that tracing the origins of food is like genealogy and that many great stories can be uncovered. Six years ago, he started curating the blog *Dann Woellert the Food Etymologist*. He's been a historical tour guide for the Cincinnati Preservation Association and on the boards of the Over-the-Rhine Museum and the Delhi Historical Society Museum. He's created food video shorts for the German Heritage Museum and is active with the German American Citizens League, the Brewery District and the Ohio 9th: A Living History. He is a five-time recipient of the Ohioana Award for Literary and Artistic Achievement.

Visit us at
www.historypress.com